THE MASK OF DECEPTION

THE MASK OF DECEPTION

Voodoo and How It Hides in a Well Known Religion

First Edition

TESTIMONY
PUBLISHING

Marisol Pareja

Copyright © 2015 Marisol Pareja

Author's products are available at special quantity discounts for bulk purchases for sales promotions, premiums, fund-raising, and educational needs. For details, write The Mask of Deception 1264 North Lakeview Drive #J411 Anaheim, CA 92807.

The Mask of Deception by Marisol Pareja

Non-Fiction

This book, or ebook, or parts thereof may not be reproduced in any form, stored in a retrieval system, or transmitted in any form by any means – electronic, mechanical, photocopy, recording, or otherwise – without prior written consent and permission of the author except in the case of brief quotations in articles and reviews as provided by the United States of America copyright law.

Copyright © 2015 Marisol Pareja *The Mask of Deception*. All rights reserved

Visit the book's website at:

www.themaskofdeception.org

Library of Congress Cataloging-in-Publication Data

Pareja, Marisol.

The Mask of Deception/Marisol Pareja.

Print Book - ISBN: 978-0-9967338-0-9

E-Book - ISBN: 978-0-9967338-1-6

LCCN: 2014916992

Editors – Brother Joseph Martinez and Christina Pareja

While the author has made every effort to provide accurate Internet addresses at the time of publication, neither the publisher nor the author assumes responsibilities for errors or for changes that occur after publication. This book has been translated into Spanish under the title La Mascara de Decepción Copyright © by Marisol Pareja. All rights reserved.

Unless otherwise noted, all Scripture is taken from the KJV (King James Version, Copyright used by permission. All rights reserved). This book is written based on a true account of the author's life.

Please, consider requesting that your local library branch purchase a copy of this volume.

Printed in the United States of America

Author Interviews, please contact us at (877) 740-4367

"For God sent not his Son into the world to condemn the world; but that the world through him might be saved."
John 3:17 King James Version (KJV)

Acknowledgements

Hello and may God bless all who read this book. I would like to thank Jesus for saving me. I feel blessed for his teaching and communicating with me while writing this book. You knew me before I was born, you protect me, and have shown me unwavering mercy and patience. I could never imagine my life without You. YOU are WORTHY of all praise and glory!

I would also like to thank God for all the answered prayers in my life; they have given me the faith to continue. I thank Jesus for saving and healing me and not forsaking me in my time of need. I also thank him for coming to my rescue and saving me.

Thank you for my family, who I love dearly, and for my beautiful mom, who was my other spiritual guide throughout the years. I would like to thank the Holy Ghost for speaking to my heart and guiding me since I became born again. All of them had a part in my life. I thank all the Pastors who have taught me so much of God's beautiful word. I thank my Brother in Christ Joseph Martinez and my sister Christina for helping me with the editing.

Thank you Father in heaven, for the honor of being able to write a book to glorify you. It has been a worthwhile task, and I have enjoyed every moment.

I surrender and lay down my life for you Lord, just as you did for me. In honor of Jesus Christ, so that all may see the glory of the good news: That you suffered, died, were buried, and rose from the dead on the third day to save all of those who would receive your selfless act of love. Over five hundred eyewitnesses saw you after your resurrection, for 40 consecutive days here on earth. Afterward, you ascended into heaven and are seated at the right hand of the Father. You are coming back soon to judge the living, and the dead and your kingdom will have no end; I eagerly await your glorious return, my Lord, what a glorious day it will be to spend eternity with you.

Contents

Chapter 1: God's Confirmation To Me 1
Chapter 2: God's Redemption For Mankind 13
Chapter 3: God's Authority on Earth 25
Chapter 4: King Jesus, Not the Easter Bunny 43
Chapter 5: The Mask of Deception 53
Chapter 6: Guilty by Association 87
Chapter 7: Mary, Co-Redeemer? 131
Chapter 8: Second Vatican Council 137
Chapter 9: Come Out Of Her, My People 153
Chapter 10: The Key To Breaking Free 167
Chapter 11: Re-Establishing Communion With God 179
More Information 185
Notes 187
Index 197

AUTHOR NOTES

HAVE YOU EVER wanted to hear from God? Could not one word from God change our lives forever? I know it changed the course of my life forever back in 2009! Trapped in religion, I saw no light at the end of the tunnel and no hope.

Right now, you may be in the same situation I was in back then. I could not break free from the circumstances I was in, and I could not understand why. I was trapped, and in bondage to Satan and I saw no way out. Then, a friend took me to church one Sunday afternoon, and the Holy Ghost convicted me of my anger through the pastor's message about anger. I had a lot of anger inside of me because of all that I had been put through, and this message woke me up. Two weeks after that message, I rededicated my life to Jesus Christ, and it has never been the same; my life changed forever. Jesus stretched out his hand and went after his prodigal daughter.

I began listening to God in that year, 2009, and as the years passed, I started hearing more and more. In September of that year, with approximately five hundred other believers, I was baptized on the Fort Lauderdale beach with my local Christian Church. It was the most memorable day of my entire life. I felt like it was a rebirth, my new beginning, and I felt as if I married Jesus Christ that day. As I came up out of the water, I walked over to where my family and friends were and on my way there I began picking up the garbage that was on the sand. When I asked the Pastor why I did this, he said it was a symbol that God was going to remove the trash from my life.

Many people I used to be friends with, God removed from my life because he was going to bring new people who would make my walk with Jesus better. Many people I loved very much I had to give up, and it was hard for me because some were family members, and some were friends. The most painful person I had to give up was a man I had been in love with for many years, he is the one who took me to church again, but it just never worked out and the Lord told me he was in my past now.

I thought differently, and when I tried to sin as I had before, I felt sorrow in my heart. I knew it was wrong, and I could no longer do the sins I used to do. I never felt that before; the Holy Ghost continually convicted my heart until I shed all my former sins. I am a completely changed person. Since then, I have heard from God on several occasions. We get to know Jesus more as we read our Bible. Therefore, if you are having a hard time with sin and are stuck in a cycle, the best thing you can do is ask Jesus to save you and go get baptized.

God instructed me to write this book in May of 2014. He also tells me what foods I should eat (I admit I am not always obedient when it comes to food) and leads me to pray as well because now he lives inside of me.

I would like to help you hear from God for yourself, if you don't already hear from him. To do so we have to get you plugged into God first.

You may wonder why most people do not hear from God. I have heard time after time people who blame God for everything bad that happens in their lives. When I asked how their relationship with God is, the answer is usually non-existent. Many have no relationship with their creator, and this is one reason we do not hear from him. We have to plug into him by reading our Bible to begin hearing him.

At the same time, when something good happens, we do not thank him. Many are disconnected from their creator, and many miss the purpose for which God placed them here. We should ask

Jesus to save us and ask him to come and live inside of us so that our prayers are answered and so that he can begin to hear our prayers. Once we do, we become co-heirs with Jesus, God the Father becomes our Father, and we become his child. Then we receive his promises in our lives and then he hears our prayers.

> *"And if children, then heirs; heirs of God, and joint-heirs with Christ; if so be that we suffer with him, that we may be also glorified together."*
> *Romans 8:17 King James Version (KJV)*

> *"The righteous cry, and the Lord heareth, and delivereth them out of all their troubles."*
> *Psalm 34:17 King James Version (KJV)*

He hears and answers the prayers of HIS people, those who have already willingly accepted Jesus and have placed their faith in him, and not anything else added to this. We put on the righteousness of Jesus through faith in him as this verse states:

> *"Even the righteousness of God which is by faith of Jesus Christ unto all and upon all them that believe: for there is no difference:"*
> *Romans 3:22 King James Version (KJV)*

Jesus wraps us in his blanket of righteousness after we place our faith in him. His white blanket of protection covers us and keeps our sins hidden under his white blanket. When God the Father looks at us, he sees Jesus white blanket around us, not our ugly sins. He stands in the middle of our sin and of God the Father and says I will cover them with my blanket. He is our mediator, and there is no other mediator or intercessor selected by God the Father, it was only Jesus Christ. Therefore, any other mediator you choose will not suffice the covering of your sins. It is for this reason why we must place our faith in Jesus alone.

> *"For there is one God, and one mediator between God and men, the man Christ Jesus;"*
> *1 Timothy 2:5 King James Version (KJV)*

If you have not already done so, this may be the primary reason you are not hearing from him. Many go to psychics and mediums because they do not hear directly from God. Many turn to statues and saints, but only one can cover our sins and that is Jesus Christ. Once we accept Jesus, we can start to hear from him on our own. We cannot mix worship of saints and worship of Jesus; He does not receive this type of worship.

Another reason we do not hear from God is that others have lain to us from the day we were born. The media lies to us, our enemies lie to us, and even family and friends lie to us. In essence, the truth is hard to see because our eyes have been closed. Therefore, when presented with the truth, we do not immediately see it. Honestly, the truth sometimes is too hard to bear, and we choose to believe the lies that we hear even though we know in our hearts that they may not be true.

Humans detect lies with only 54 percent accuracy. A 2006 academic study that involved 24,000 individual judgments of lies and truths found our mean performance to be 54 percent. Between 75 percent and 82 percent of lies go undetected, according to deception researchers Aldert Vrij and Bella DePaulo.

A study published in the American Psychologist found that only members of the U.S. Secret Service consistently fared better than the average person's 54 percent accuracy. My point in mentioning this is that unless we research your subject in depth, the chances of deception are higher according to this research.

The Bible also tells us to wake up and not let others deceive us.

> *"And that, knowing the time, that now it is high time to awake out of sleep: for now is our salvation nearer than when we believed."*
> Romans 13:11 King James Version (KJV)

The only thing that arouses us from the slumber of deception is to understand the time we are living in so that we can prepare for what is to take place.

Another form of deception is commingling truth with error. This form of deception makes it harder to decipher the truth from the lie. It is this mixing of truth with error that is most used by the Satan. If the adversary removes a sentence or two from the Bible or changes even just one word to change the overall meaning, it gets confusing. Satan, our enemy, comes as a wolf in sheep's clothing; he hides behind a pretense of goodness.

Would we drink a glass of poison willingly? Nobody would be that crazy. However, if someone were to give us a glass of orange juice with a few drops of poison in it, we will just drink it and not notice the poison until we are dead. In this way, the devil does not give us pure error; he mixes it with some truth and serves it to us, and it becomes difficult to taste the poison. The consequences are still the same, our death. Satan is the master of subtlety, which by definition means:

> "Hard to notice or see; not obvious."

He takes that which is true and makes a counterfeit of the real, which results in the ultimate deception. What is the definition of 'counterfeit'? According to Merriam Webster, the definition of counterfeit is as follows:

"Made to look like an exact copy of something in order to trick people"

Satan mimicks everything God has to create a counterfeit so real, it would be difficult to decipher if you have not studied it closely. This is the very nature of deception; for every truth that God has, the adversary has a counterfeit reality. If God has a Church, then Satan has his church. Satan even has followers who call themselves saints, just as God has servants called saints. If God has angels, Satan has angels. If God has Holy Scriptures, then Satan has his bible. If God has a sacred day, Satan has his holy day. Do you understand my point? He creates a counterfeit so close to the real church that it becomes difficult to tell them apart. The Catholic Church is the one he uses most, and its foundations are feable and based on idolatry and necromancy. Satan leads to confusion, and Satan – not God - is the author of confusion.

The commingling of truth with error is the subtelty that Satan uses to deceive his followers into worshiping him and his fallen angels. The statues tie people to the natural realm, eliminating the superiorness of God and our need to look up. It forces us to look here on earth for answers, instead of up to God. I was not given Satan's tactics until I began writing this book, that God revealed this truth to me. It was still hidden from my eyes, even though I was delivered from the power of darkness and born again.

"And no Marvel; for Satan himself is transformed into an angel of light. Therefore it is no great thing if his ministers also be transofrmed as the ministers of righteousness; whose end shall be according to their works"
2 Corinthians 11:14-15 King James Version (KJV)

The closer Satan comes to the truth, by mixing that truth with a bit of error, the more credible he seems. A good counterfeit would be very difficult to tell apart from the real thing. We would have to study the subject and do some in-depth research. I am here to tell you that I have done this research, and what God has shown me is astounding.

Many of us do not hear from God because we have chosen to believe the lies told to us, instead of searching for the truth with all of our hearts. Some have opted to take the blue pill instead of the red pill; some have chosen to be numb to the truth instead of searching for the truth as Neo did in the film 'The Matrix'. It is when we search for the truth (and find it), that we find freedom.

Another reason we do not hear from God is, of course, sin. Sin separated Adam and Eve from God, and they died (Spiritually) the day they chose to listen to Satan instead of God.

Once we receive Jesus and call on his name, and ask him to forgive us, our sins are wiped away. Asking for forgiveness, and asking Jesus into our spirit opens the lines of communication between God and us again. It is that simple!

Satan's great goal is to stop us from knowing the real Jesus because he knows once we have Jesus; Satan's power in our lives is broken. Satan makes salvation seem so hard to attain by claiming we must work for it and earn it through works, baptism, confirmation, and communion. In reality, salvation is received by asking God for it and receiving the gift, he already gave to us, Jesus.

"For by grace are ye saved through faith; and that not of yourselves: it is the gift of God: Not of works, lest any man should boast."
Ephesians 2:8-9 King James Version (KJV)

It cannot be any clearer than the verse above. When we begin to read the Bible and believe God's word over Satan's lies, then our lives begin to improve, and our children become blessed for many generations to come.

> *"Know therefore that the Lord thy God, he is God, the faithful God, which keepeth covenant and mercy with them that love him and keep his commandments to a thousand generations;"*
> *Deuteronomy 7:9 King James Version (KJV)*

Since my salvation, God healed me of TMJ, arthritis, chronic bronchitis, smoking, fornication, and a tooth infection. More importantly, he has healed my mind.

He has given me wisdom beyond anything I could have learned on my own. I had no idea I was idol worshiping or offending God when I worshiped idols because that is what I was taught. I know many who practice today who were given the same information as I was, a complete lie. I believed Voodoo was from God because that is what they told me. I also grew up in a Catholic home with a stepmother who was into occult practices. I saw nothing wrong with it because I saw my stepmother practiced it. Blinded to the truth, I knew whose side I wanted to be on at the age of twenty-nine, but I still could not see the entire truth.

Some psychics, mediums, and spiritists are friendly people who have been lied to by the devil. They were probably seeking God and the enemy crossed their path at the right moment and stuck his foot out to trip them. Convincing them to use their God-given gifts under the wrong anointing. We need to be under God's anointing, not the adversaries.

Whatever religion you are in more than likely passed down from your parents. We must ask ourselves, whether the religion we are in allows us to hear from God about the direction of our lives. Does your God give you wonderful promises for you, your children and the generations to come? Does he back them up with answered prayers that you can see happening in the world and your family life daily? More importantly, are you choosing Jesus over your religion, or are you choosing your religion over Jesus? Do you know with 100% certainty, that when you die you will go to heaven? If not, then keep reading and let me help you to know my God, the God of Isaac, Abraham, and Jacob. His name is YHVH or YAHWEH—among many other names, such as Jehovah. The only true God of the entire universe.

> *"I am the LORD, and there is none else, there is no God beside me: I girded thee, though thou hast not known me: That they may know from the rising of the sun, and from the west, that there is none beside me. I am the LORD, and there is none else."*
> *Isaiah 45:5-6 King James Version (KJV)*

My goal is to help you begin hearing from God and to present you with the truth so that you can move from the counterfeit to the truth if that is where you find yourself. I hope to encourage you to read the Bible daily and teach you how to begin praying daily so that you too can have fellowship with God.

> *"Jesus saith unto him, I am the way, the **truth**, and the life: no man cometh unto the Father, but by me."*
> *John 14:6 King James Version (KJV)*

If you have worshiped any God other than Jesus, it means you have other lovers. Jesus wants you for himself. He is the one who created you, he is the one pursuing you now through this book, and he is the one who suffered and died for you and rose from the dead for you so that you would come to him. The Bible says that God is a jealous God, and he wants you all for himself.

> *"For thou shalt worship no other god: for the LORD, whose name is Jealous, is a jealous God:"*
> *Exodus 34:14 King James Version (KJV)*

I am sure you have researched in great depths your religion, and you believe it to be the truth. But I know it is possible to sit in a pew swallowing information without thinking about whether it is true or not. I know this because that is where I was. Maybe some of you are in the same situation I used to be in. Maybe, you were raised in a religion because of your parents, and you've never stopped to ask whether God is pleased with that. If you are weary and fed up with doing life on your own, Jesus says to lay all your burdens upon him.

> *"Come unto me, all ye that labour and are heavy laden, and I will give you rest."*
> *Matthew 11:28 King James Version (KJV)*

Obeying one of the most important commandments God gave us will set you, your family, and even entire nations free. The commandment I am speaking of is the second commandment, in which God tells us not to make any graven images, nor to bow down to them, nor to serve them. There is a reason God made this one of the first four commandments, and it is a crucial one to him. Did you know this is the only commandment the Catholic Church has removed from their doctrine?

The first four commandments deal with our relationship with God, therefore, if we sin against our Maker by breaking one of them, we will be out of fellowship with him. It is offensive to Jesus when we bow down to a fabricated statue and call it a god. He bled to death for us and was spat on, mocked, beaten and crucified so that we would not have to pay for our sins. Making a statue and worshiping it instead of him is idolatry, and it greatly saddens him.

If you died in somebodies place and he or she honored someone or something else instead of you, how would you feel? It hurts

Jesus so much to see how misled we are by man-made rules and traditions—He even wrote several verses saying so:

> *"Ye shall not add unto the word which I command you, neither shall ye diminish ought from it, that ye may keep the commandments of the Lord your God which I command you"*
> *Deuteronomy 4:2 King James Version (KJV)*
>
> ~
>
> *"What thing so ever I command you, observe to do it: thou shalt not add thereto, nor diminish from it."*
> *Deuteronomy 12:32 King James Version (KJV)*
>
> ~
>
> *"And if any man shall take away from the words of the book of this prophecy, God shall take away his part out of the book of life, and out of the holy city, and from the things which are written in this book."*
> *Revelation 22:19 King James Version (KJV)*

As we can see, and may have already known, plenty of verses in the Bible tell us that we do not have the ability to change God's Word. If we do, he says we will be taken out of the book of life all together meaning we will go to hell.

Humans also cannot make higher beings, so those statues cannot do anything for us. The idols we worship are made in a factory and painted with human hands; they are not supernatural in any way. God, on the other hand, wants us to turn to him and speak to him instead of these idols so we can watch how supernatural our life truly becomes.

It is ridiculous to think we can create a god out of statues and pray to them and believe that they can answer us. Humans cannot create higher beings. We deceive ourselves when we begin to think that we can. Freedom and blessings come when we give up our idols.

Sadly, because of their worship of hundreds of strange gods, countries like Cuba, and China remain in captivity by their governments and their children are cursed, according to God's Word. The Word of God is flawless as stated in the Bible in the following verses and no human being on earth has the authority to change it for any reason whatsoever:

> *"The words of the LORD are pure words: as silver tried in a furnace of earth, purified seven times."*
> *Psalm 12:6 King James Version (KJV)*

~

> *"For ever, O Lord, thy word is settled in heaven.*
> *Psalm 119:89 King James Version (KJV)*

~

> *"Every Word of God is pure: he is a shield unto them that put their trust in him. Add thou not unto his words, lest he reprove thee, and thou be found a liar"*
> *Proverbs 30:5-6 King James Version (KJV)*

There are certain organizations in the world today that say they are infallible and have the authority to change the Bible, but the proof that this is not the case is found in the scriptures mentioned previously. We are to believe God and not the men of this world just as Eve should have obeyed God and not Satan in the Garden of Eden.

Jesus was the only human being who did not sin, ever! Since his ascension into heaven, there has not been even one human being without sin, not even Mary. To say that we are without sin is a sin because we are calling God a liar in doing so.

> *"For all have sinned, and come short of the glory of God."*
> *Romans 3:23 King James Version (KJV)*

God wrote the Ten Commandments with his finger on stone tablets. I believe that they were important to him, if he wrote them with his finger. He does not approve of any human being removing or altering them, adding anything to them, or removing anything from them.

Only someone being deceived by the devil would try to say that he could change God's commandments. We must pray that such people learn the truth. The reason God cast Satan and one-third of his angels out of heaven was because of Satan's pride. He wanted to raise himself higher than God did. Satan was so ingenious that he even convinced other angels to fall with him.

If Satan can deceive angels who are higher beings with extraordinary powers, he can certainly deceive us humans. We rely on our emotions and are so needy and we need guidance for everything. It is almost too good to be true for him. Satan has created several hundred religions, just to make the true church unrecognizable.

I will show you how he has done so in the chapters to come. In the meantime, keep reading and I will walk you through how and why we should give up idol worshiping, provide evidence that it is God's will, and reveal the benefits we receive for doing so. Once we are born again of the Spirit of Jesus, he lives in us and we begin hearing from God. We open ourselves up to receive the many blessings he has in store for us, our families, and the nations that receive him.

I would also like to add, that this book is not directed against any individual inparticular, instead it is a critique of the Catholic institution as a whole. It is based on my personal experience with both religions that I expose in this book. It is with much love that I provide this information and is not an attack on any person in particular. There are millions of wonderful Catholics who may be truly saved, but cannot see the entire truth, just like what happened to me. I feel it is my duty as a saved follower of Jesus to provide this information out of love for my fellow brothers and sisters in Christ. To help them and not hinder them and to show them what God has shown me. A way for them to gain insight from my pain and sufferings, and a way of escape for the dark times that are coming if you are not on the right side.

I hope you will join me in worshiping the one true God, who is accessible and will listen to us when we call him. In chapter one, I walk you through the process of how God instructed me to write this book—that is a pretty supernatural story.

Chapter 1:

God's Confirmation To Me

"Ask, and it shall be given you; seek, and ye shall find; knock, and it shall be opened unto you:
For every one that asketh receiveth; and he that seeketh findeth; and to him that knocketh it shall
be opened"
Matthew 7:7 King James Version (KJV)

IT IS WITHOUT a shadow of a doubt that God told me to write this book. One day in the middle of June 2014, I called a prayer line that I often call to pray. A friend I love dearly was lost and needed salvation.

We learn from the Bible that when two or more come into agreement in the name of Jesus, he is guaranteed to hear and be there.

> "For where two or three are gathered together in my name, there am I in the midst of them."
> Matthew 18:20 King James Version (KJV)

After the prayer partner had prayed for my friend's salvation and we were about to hang up, there was a moment of silence. She said, "Hold on a minute—God is telling me something." She got my attention; I waited for her to speak again. She said, "The Lord is telling me something about a book." I was astonished, mostly because I had already thought of writing a book and had many portions written already. I had called this line many times over a period of the last three years—but this had never happened before. The Bible says that we must be willing to give everyone up for him in the following verse:

> "He that loveth father or mother more than me is not worthy of me: and he that loveth son or daughter more than me is not worthy of me."
> Matthew 10:37 King James Version (KJV)

I accepted Jesus when I was 29 years old, but I did not surround myself with other believers because I didn't realize the importance of doing so, and consequently I backslid for many years. I feel that my actual conversion occurred at the age of 39, just five months before my 40th birthday. God often works in numbers, and 40 is a time of testing. I began working on the book immediately. If there is anything I have learned throughout my years as a believer that when God tells us to do something, that we should not hesitate. This book has taken me one year and three months to complete. The significant point is that I wrote two books in one, unknowingly.

I almost lost my life once because I did not listen to God, so now I always try my very best to immediately do whatever the Holy Ghost tells me. I explain how I almost lost my life in detail in my other book: *My Escape from Organized Religion* released in September 2016. From the beginning to the end of the writing process, the Lord brought me everyone and everything that I needed to complete this book.

I had never written a book before but, once I started, I loved it. I remember thinking that I could have achieved it long before. So if you have ever felt a nudge from God to write a book, do it! Do not hesitate, as it could be the most significant outreach you do for him and his kingdom because of the many people it can reach all over the world.

I enjoyed receiving information from God. Some nights he would speak to my heart, with clarity; other times, he would convey his message in a dream. On other occasions, he would place an idea in my head while I was watching a show or documentary on television. Only two days after praying with the prayer partner, I received an email from a nationally renowned Christian copywriter. The subject line said, *'How to Write a Book in 30 Days or Less.'*

I watched his webcast and signed up for his training immediately. I had never heard of this man before and did not understand how he found my email address, but his training provided the starting point I needed for my book. In his training, he teaches that the title and the book cover are the most important part of any book, so I asked the Lord for the title of my book shortly after that.

On the same evening during which I prayed for a title, I had a dream that I was with a man I had never met before. He looked like an ordinary man: he wore regular clothing and seemed like a friend. After we had traveled to several locations throughout the neighborhood together, we went into an apartment and stood in the kitchen. His back was facing me, and when he turned around to look at me, all of a sudden he was wearing a white mask. I woke up startled and thought, "What could that possibly mean?" I discussed the dream with a family member, but neither of us was able to decipher its meaning.

As I watched more of the copywriter's webinar training, I found my answer. The training provided a website offering pre-made book covers, and as I skimmed through the covers, I saw one featuring an illustration of a mask exactly like the one in my dream. I instantly knew that the dream's purpose was to provide the title that God wanted for my book. Initially, I thought of titling it The Mask until my mother pointed out that there were already too many movies and books by that name. After all, I did not want my book to be confused with past novels or comedy films! She suggested the title The Mask of Deception. Her suggestion was the missing piece that I needed.

About a year prior to when God asked me to write the book I also heard him tell me, "Let me take care of you." I humbly accepted and prayed for him to provide a way. After all, what better offer can any of us receive than God Almighty telling us he will take care of us? I remember feeling an almost inexplicably high sense of security after that. While at a church in Fullerton, California, I heard him instructing me to lay it all down for him. He wanted me to serve him in ministry full time.

Around that same time period, the Lord spoke through me to reach a Catholic man. I hired him to help me move some personal items out of a storage unit in California. The family member who was with me that day and I asked the man to come to our church in Fullerton as it was near Easter time, and the church was having a huge event there.

He said he already had a church and told me that he was a Christian, baptized into a Christian church and was led into a Catholic Church shortly thereafter. With no prior knowledge of what I was saying, I told him that back in the old days when witches were burned at the stake, Voodoo priests had to hide their practice to avoid being killed, so they opened a church, called it Christian, and practiced Voodoo in secret. I told him that today they are known today as the Catholic Church. Back in ancient times some Kings were obedient to God's word and they killed witches according to the following commandment in the old testament:

> "Thou shalt not suffer a witch to live."
> Exodus 22:18 King James Version (KJV)

After I had witnessed to this man, I realized that I did not know how I obtained the information I gave him; the words just came out of my mouth. I pondered later that evening and asked myself where I received that information.

In ancient times, practitioners of Voodoo could not practice their faith openly as they do today. They had to hide their religion so they would not get burnt at the stake. Therefore, they opened a church, called it Christian, and held services on Sundays to further mask its deception. These Voodoo priests hid under a pretense of good so they would not die, and this is how the Catholic Church had its start, although they will more than likely never admit to it. In the evenings, they practiced idol worshiping, necromancy[1] and the calling up and worshiping of the dead—as

---

[1] Communicating with the dead.

is their custom even to this day when they canonize church members.

They even built cemeteries and entire cities beneath these churches so that they could have easy access to human bones and body parts—which is what they use in Voodoo. They told the church members that these crypts were to bury the poor who had no money for a funeral. Again, they appeared to be good Samaritans, as was their custom. Having these crypts at their disposal, would be easier than going into a cemetery, digging up the remains of human body parts and bones, and risk getting caught stealing people's organs and limbs like they do today.

One of the several incidents I read about is of two Voodoo priestesses returning from Cuba, who were found with the remains of human skulls hidden in their pottery.[2] Another incident was a case in Chicago, Illinois in which eighteen human heads with the skin still intact were discovered on a flight from Rome, Italy, where the Vatican leads its church.

During the time I was telling this Catholic man about the origin of the Catholic Church, I could see that what I was telling him scared him a lot—because he stepped back and almost tripped over. I finally learned where the Lord wanted me to concentrate my ministry. As I began researching the topic a little more, I found that there were 1.2 billion Catholics worldwide, and more than 60 million Voodoo and Santeria practitioners. Santeria is a pantheistic Afro-Cuban religious cult developed from the beliefs and customs of the Yoruba people in Africa are also synchronized with Catholicism as Author Leslie Desmangles writes in her book *Faces of the Gods: Vodou and Roman Catholicism*.

---

[2] *The Wire* April 24, 2013, 5:41 pm Apr 24, 2013, 5:41 PM *Human Skulls Have a Habit of Popping Up at Florida Airports.*

CHAPTER 1: GOD'S CONFIRMATION TO ME

Voodoo is a black religious cult practiced in the Caribbean and the southern US, combining elements of Roman Catholicism ritual with traditional African magical and religious rites. I became determined to make this information known to the entire world and make a dent in those numbers. I want to expose the truth because the truth does, set us free and the Bible tells us to shine the light on darkness and reprove it in the following verse:

"And have no fellowship with the unfruitful works of darkness, but rather reprove them."
Ephesians 5:11 King James Version (KJV)

I felt a deep sorrow in my heart for those misled by this church, mostly for the children. I was once one of those children and, had I known then what I know today, much of the misery I experienced growing up could have been prevented. Many unclean, familiar spirits linger in these churches. Let me give you an example of what happened to me.

I grew up having TMJ, which is temporamandibular joint dysfunction, a nervous condition in which you clench your jaws while you sleep. I had clenched my teeth so much since I was little that I ground the jawbone down to the point that I had a click in my jaw when I opened my mouth. I believe this was a spirit that caused me to do this, and it came from the Catholic Church and the unclean spirits in that church. The reason I believe this is because, after I was born again, both the clenching and the clicking have gone away. I no longer suffer from the pains in my jaw that I used to have. I firmly believe that a lot of sickness and disease comes from the unclean spirits hiding in these churches—and the people cannot see it.

It is also my belief that, each time we walk into a Catholic Church or any of the churches that are the offspring of it, we are walking out with many unclean spirits and demons. Spirits of the dead linger in Catholic Churches because they are what they worship. It is my firm belief that we take them home with us. They like to cling on to people and personal items in our home.

They secretly wreak havoc in our homes and are the leading cause of infidelity, physical abuse, children's nightmares, TMJ, and many other diseases. Each one of them serves a different purpose, and all hinder us and our families in some way. The Bible calls them unclean or familiar spirits.

The reason I believe this is because several years after I had been born again, I became friends with a Catholic family. I stayed at their home one night to babysit for them, and I had the same spirit attack me as when I was a little girl and lived with my dad and stepmother. Not to mention, this couples marriage ended in divorce. This is no coincidence; I believe it is directly related to the spirits people bring home from entering these churches.

Another reason I suspect the spirits attach themselves to non-believers is because several times I have spoken over the telephone to my family members who are Catholic, I can feel the spirits on them. They come through the phone and give me headaches. I pray, of course, and they are removed, but it has happened each time I speak with one of them. Unfortunately, I have had to sever friendships with many of them due to this reason and I continue to pray for them in private.

During the time I was writing this book, I remembered my family in South America from my dad's side. I felt determined to tell them this truth so that they could decide what they wanted to do with this information. I hoped that they would, at the very least, know who the head of their church is and that it is not Jesus Christ as they claim.

It was not until several months after I spoke to the Catholic man in California that I was inspired to do more research at the local library. I researched synchronicity between Catholicism and Voodoo. Seeking more proof, I checked out all the books I could on Voodoo. I also checked out all the books on Catholicism. As I read them, I found the two religions had much in common.

My parents raised me as a Catholic; I accepted Jesus in a Christian church of my free will at age eighteen. I fell into the occult practices of Voodoo at the age of thirty-three because I was so deceived back then. I believed that Voodoo was from God like they told me. Jesus Christ has been with me every step of the way, even when I was a little girl. I learned throughout my journey that being Catholic does not save us from hell. If being Catholic delivers us from the powers of darkness, then why, when my mom died giving birth to my youngest brother in 1976, did the Lord send her back down to earth? He did not know her, and still had mercy on her and sent her back down so that my siblings and I could get saved. At that time, she was a Catholic, and so were we.

Here is her powerful testimony of when she died and came back at the mercy of Almighty God:

> *"When I was in the hospital, and the doctor was delivering my last child, I was under anesthesia (knocked out) and I was taken up by no power of my own, and very fast, but pleasant, in the dark and then toward a light and was placed in mid-air.*
>
> *The reason I was placed in mid-air was that I was in a spiritual world and not in a physical one. My spirit could see, feel, hear, and think. Moreover, I thought to myself and said aloud, "Where am I?" Then, at that moment, I heard a sound of water that was speaking, but I could not understand what it was saying. Then a being came very close to me. I could not see him, but I felt him, and he was piercing through me to read my life and thoughts, probably because I was a spirit. This entity then went away for a few minutes, as a few*

minutes would be in the spirit world, and asked me this question. "And what judgment shall I have for you?" The voice was gentle, but firm.

I wondered to myself whether my husband would be able to care for my other three children and this new baby on his own. I guess I decided he would. Therefore, I answered and said, "Whatever judgment you have for me, is what I have to accept." Then that same being that pierced through me before came back and filled me with warmth, and a loving feeling you never feel on this earth. It was total unconditional love. I turned to see where the light was coming from and was blacked out and woke up in my hospital room, in intensive care, and was hooked up for electric shock.

The baby was a cesarean birth. I came home from the hospital, and everything was normal and the experience I had I did not remember, but my mother-in-law said to me when I walked in the door, "You died."

I did not think anything of it. 20 years later, while the son I delivered that day was reading a verse from the Bible, the same feelings, sounds, and thoughts I had experienced twenty years before, I was experiencing again.

One week later, I went to my cousin's church and was born again and baptized. I honestly believe the reason God let me come back was because he wanted me to be saved, and I was the only one who could come back and accept Jesus in the physical world and help my children do the same. Since then all of my kids have been born again, praise God.

He gave me the proof that I needed to know that he was real. My son was born again also on that same day.
LOVE Mom"

CHAPTER 1: GOD'S CONFIRMATION TO ME

Baptism, doing good deeds, keeping the Catholic sacraments, or trying to keep the Ten Commandments, or praying to Mary and obeying the Pope do not get us into heaven—nor do they save us. If all of these things could save us than why would Jesus, have to come to save us? Nothing but belief in Jesus Christ saves us.

> *"For by grace are ye saved through faith; and that not of yourselves: it is the gift of God:"*
> *Ephesians 2:8 King James Version (KJV)*

In the following chapter, I explain God's plan of reconciliation for humanity and then provide proof that the Bible was sent by God to humanity so that we can get to heaven. God does not lie, so every word in the Bible is correct and, once we begin to believe every word, God begins to show up in our lives.

I also provide biblical evidence that no man on earth has the authority to change God's words or commandments; even though there are some who say they do have that authority.

Chapter 2:

God's Redemption For Mankind

"For the wages of sin is death; but the gift of God is eternal life through Jesus Christ our Lord."
Romans 6:23 King James Version (KJV)

IT IS IMPORTANT that we understand what Jesus did for us and why so that we can better understand his love for us. We need him, whether you realize it or not.

When Adam and Eve sinned, they were separated from God because he is a Holy God and only Holy people and angels can be near him. To preserve his kingdom, God cannot allow sin into heaven. When Lucifer (Satan), who was God's created servant, had evil thoughts in his heart against God, he was cast out of heaven to the earth along with one-third of the other angels who sided with Satan.

> "And there was war in heaven: Michael and his angels fought against the dragon; and the dragon fought and his angels, and prevailed not: neither was their place found anymore in heaven. And the great dragon was cast out, that old serpent, called the Devil, and Satan, which deceiveth the whole world: he was cast out into the earth, and his angels were case out with him.
> Revelation 12:7-12 King James Version (KJV)

As we can see from the above verse, Satan is no match for God and his angels, and we also see that Satan was cast down to earth. From my prior experience in the occult I believe that today, Satan lives in a main host human body and is the man I was to be initiated under in voodoo. He told me that an entity took over his body in 1980 and he has had no control of his body ever since. Satan leaves this host body when he needs to and possesses different people when he needs to, in order to accomplish his will on earth. Voodoo and Santeria initiates are people willing to allow "spirits" to mount them or possess them.

Mount is the term they use, so as not to scare their initiates by saying possession. It is demon possession and they willingly allow Satan to take control over their bodies, thinking they are Christian spirits. Satan tells them it is just a spirit, but it is not; it is either Satan or one of his fallen angels that he has called up from hell... to help him do evil.

As we can see, these practices are far from being of a Godly nature and humans should not allow any spirit to take over their body for any reason. God never actually allowed me to be initiated into Voodoo; I was just there to be a witness as I never learned any spells or anything like that and much less allow a spirit to take over my body.

For humans to be able to approach God again after sin was transferred to us by Adam and Eve's disobedience, there must be blood atonement for sin. God's law requires blood to atone for or pay for sin so that we can be near to God again and for him to hear our prayers.

In the book of Hebrews, God explains to us that each year on the Day of Atonement, the high priest entered the Holy of Holies and sprinkled the blood of animals sacrificed for the atonement of the sins of God's people. The priest sprinkled the blood on the mercy seat of God on the Ark of the Covenant. The point conveyed by this imagery is that it is only through the offering of blood that the condemnation of the law could be taken away and violations of God's laws covered. Sin was paid for in the old covenant by animal sacrifice—the blood of an animal.

In God's new covenant, Jesus Christ pays for sin. God loved us so much that he wanted us to be able to come to him again. Therefore, he sent his only son to be the sacrifice for all humanity's sin.

> *"For God so loved the world that he gave his only begotten Son, that whosoever believeth in him should not perish, but have everlasting life."*
> John 3:16 King James Version (KJV)

Since God is a just God, Satan and his angels will never enter heaven again because salvation is for human beings, not angels.

Satan hates us because of this and does anything in his power to make us focus on anything or anyone besides Jesus so that we go to hell with him. He is the serpent that bites the horse's heels so that the rider shall fall backward.

> *"Dan shall be a serpent by the way, an adder in the path that biteth the horse heels, so that his rider shall fall backward."*
> *Genesis 49:17 King James Version(KJV)*

Those humans who believe in Jesus, they go to heaven when they die and those who do not will go to hell. When Jesus was dying on the cross, one of the thieves next to him repented and asked him for mercy. Jesus replied:

> *"And Jesus said unto him, Verily I say unto thee, Today shalt thou be with me in paradise"*
> *Luke 23:43 King James Version (KJV)*

The thief on the cross was never baptized or confirmed, never took communion, never participated in Ash Wednesday, nor did he become a member of the Catholic Church. The thief was saved strictly, because he repented and asked Jesus to save him, therefore proving that we must repent and ask Jesus to save us and deliver us from the powers of darkness, just as his word describes. The other criminal on Calvary did not repent, and therefore it is believed that he is in hell.

There has always been a separation of believers and unbelievers after death (Luke 16:19-31 KJV). The righteous have always gone to paradise or heaven; the wicked have always gone to hell. The first resurrection is of believers who will stand before the Judgment Seat of Christ to receive rewards based on meritorious service to him. The second resurrection will be that of unbelievers who will stand before the Great White Throne Judgment of God. At that point, all will be sent to their eternal destination.

The wicked to the lake of fire (Revelation 20:11-15 KJV), and the righteous to a new heaven and a new earth (Revelation 21 – 22 KJV).

Jesus Christ was crucified for all humanity for the remission of sins, even though he was not guilty of any crime and did not sin. He took my sin and your sin upon himself so that we would not have to pay for our sins on judgment day.

Jesus was scourged by a cat of nine tails; His skin was ripped to the bone prior to the crucifixion. He then carried his cross to Golgotha and was crucified. Crucifixion was a gruesome execution. The entire body weight is supported by the stretched arms, and extreme strain is placed on the wrists, arms, and shoulders, sometimes causing dislocation of the elbows and shoulders. It was also the most humiliating and disgraceful form of punishment, reserved for the worst law breakers.

The rib cage is constrained in a fixed position, making it extremely difficult to breathe and hard to take even one breath of air. The prisoner continually attempts to draw himself back up by his feet, to allow for inflation of the lungs, enduring terrible pain in his feet and legs. The primary cause of death by crucifixion is asphyxiation resulting from a lack of exchange of oxygen and carbon dioxide due to respiratory failure.

It is said, death by crucifixion lasts anywhere from nine hours to a few days, depending on how bad victims had been scourged. Jesus had endured six hours on the cross before he died. His quick death proves that he had been scourged more than the norm. After they had scourged him, the guards beat him and mocked him.

> *"And the men that held Jesus mocked him, and smote him."*
> *Luke 22:63 King James Version (KJV)*

~

> *"And some began to spit on him, and to cover his face, and to buffet him, and to say unto him, Prophesy: and the servants did strike him with the palms of their hands."*
> *Mark 14:65 King James Version (KJV)*

Jesus' death was how he showed us that he loved us. He died for all of us. It was the ultimate display of a loving, beautiful, and selfless God who loves his people. Those who reject him, have to pay for their own sin when they die. It is not at all, what he wants for us, but not accepting such an offering will leave him no other choice. It is by Jesus' blood sacrifice that God forgives our sin and his wrath turned away from us. Just as the Jews placed the blood on the doorpost so that they would not be killed by God's wrath, in this same manner the blood of Jesus saves those who put their trust in him.

Jesus was worshiped by thousands of angels all day and all night in heaven before he came down to earth to become a human being. Jesus left his beautiful kingdom where he had it all, just to come down and live in a human body to be beaten, mocked, and spat on by the same people for whom he was being crucified. It is unquestionably the most selfless act in all of history. The Father in heaven and Jesus the Son planned salvation from the beginning. The cross was not a failure or a surprise to God as recently claimed by the Pope to the world at St. Patrick's Cathedral New York, Thursday 24 September 2015.

This is what he said:

> *"And his life, humanly speaking, ended in failure, in the failure of the cross."*

This statement is very disrespectful to say the least. Jesus knew why he was born and what he came to do; He was born to

CHAPTER 2: GOD'S REDEMPTION FOR MANKIND

die and he knew it. The Papacy teaches that the cross was a failure as you can see above in the Pope's statement to the entire world. They think that Jesus failed his mission, but instead he fulfilled it. God does not always tell his enemies his plans, and therefore they cannot understand his words or actions.

> *"Therefore will I divide him a portion with the great, and he shall divide the spoil with the strong; because he hath poured out his soul unto death: and he was numbered with the transgressors; and he bare the sin of many, and made intercession for the transgressors."*
> *Isaiah 53:12 King James Version (KJV)*
>
> ~
>
> *"But he was wounded for our transgressions; he was bruised for our iniquities: the chastisement of our peace was upon him; and with his stripes we are healed."*
> *Isaiah 53:5 King James Version (KJV)*
>
> ~
>
> *"When Jesus therefore had received the vinegar, he said, It is finished: and he bowed his head, and gave up the ghost."*
> *John 19:30 King James Version (KJV)*

The previous verses from the Old Testament clearly predicted Jesus' future and were written prior to his birth. Then in John 19:30 Jesus said "It is Finished". Meaning he accomplished what he came to do.

Today in the twentieth century, we can fly to Jerusalem and see where Jesus was buried. There is actual proof of his existence in history. Millions of people go to Jerusalem annually just to stand where Jesus stood. He was a real person; he still heals people today. He still talks with people, and evidence that he is still answering prayers exists among all his believers all over the world. You may not see it in the Catholic Church, but you will in a Bible believing church. My point is that there is proof that he did exist, still exists, and is alive today. It is the main way to identify that Jesus is really who he claimed to be, The Messiah. The proof of millions of people's changed lives all around the world is evidence that he is the Messiah.

My own changed life is all the evidence and proof that I need to believe in him. Salvation is for everyone, not just for the Israelites, God's chosen people. We are grafted in with the Israelites when we accept Jesus and inherit all their promises.

After his death on the cross and his time in the tomb for three days, he came back to earth in his new body—a glorified body as God the Father had raised him from the dead. More than five hundred people saw him and told others what they saw. The twelve disciples saw him and were strengthened by this, and those who were doubtful finally believed. Especially doubting Thomas, as we will see in the following verses:

*"After that, he was seen of above **five hundred** brethren at once; of whom the greater part remain unto this present, but some are fallen asleep."*
1 Corinthians 15:6 King James Version (KJV)

~

"Then saith he to Thomas, Reach hither thy finger, and behold my hands; and reach hither thy hand, and thrust it into my side: and be not faithless, but believing."
John 20:27 King James Version (KJV)

~

"Behold my hands and my feet, that it is I myself: handle me, and see; for a spirit hath not flesh and bones, as ye see me have."
Luke 24:39 King James Version (KJV)

~

"And when me had so said, he shewed unto them his hands and his side. Then were the disciples glad, when they saw the Lord."
John 20:20 King James Version (KJV)

The disciples were sad when Jesus died. They thought they would never see him again and yearned for His presence. When he appeared to them, the disciples were filled with so much joy and strength—because they had seen him die and then saw him alive again. I believe it is also imperative to note that Peter, who had previously been so filled with fear when he denied Jesus three times, was now a bold witness unto death for Jesus. It was because he saw Jesus resurrected, and that gave him the strength and belief he needed to become one of the boldest witnesses for Jesus (perhaps the boldest). When the Romans at that time caught up with Peter to kill him, he asked them to crucify him upside down because he did not feel worthy to die like his Savior.

Would you like to pray to have Jesus Christ as Lord in your life? If so, we can use the prayer below. There is nothing magical in the words, but if we believe it in our hearts, God will hear us and welcome us into His family.

> "Lord Jesus, I know I have sinned, and that my sin has separated me from you. I am truly sorry. Please forgive me and save me. I believe that you died for my sins, that God raised you from the dead, and you are alive today. I receive Jesus as my Savior and Lord. Please fill me with your Spirit, and help me to obey you for the rest of my life. My life belongs to you now.
> In Jesus' name Amen."

If you have not already seen the movie *The Passion of the Christ,* I suggest you see what Jesus did for us by watching it. The Director spent $45 million of his own money to produce it independently because he had trouble-finding people who wanted to be part of a religious film. The film grossed over $600 million in revenue. He knew that doing this movie might cost him his career, but I believe that the Lord used him to bring about the most amazing depiction of Jesus's last twelve hours on earth ever created.

Then his next forty days on earth after his resurrection can be seen by watching the new movie *Risen*.

This film is an excellent message that shows us all how Jesus suffered to save us and that our souls are important enough for God to have died for them. It is also a reminder that those who do take a stand for Jesus will suffer persecution. Only two short years after *The Passion of the Christ*, the Director of the movie made him a target for the enemy and his reputation went spiraling downward. He received a lot of bad media coverage from that point forward. We are important enough for Jesus to die for, no matter how we view ourselves or what sins we have committed.

One of the adversary's biggest lies is that we can earn our salvation by works, or baptism, or keeping one of his man-made sacraments. Jesus' sacrifice was so great, that nothing we do could ever suffice—no amount of good could make up for the death of the Son of God—works cannot get us into heaven. Placing our faith and trust in Jesus and turning from our sin on the other hand, will. Satan also deceives some people into thinking he does not exist and tells those who practice Voodoo and Santeria that their religion is from God, when it is not.

Do not let the adversary convince you that you are not good enough. The devil lies to people and influences them to believe that they have been too evil for God to forgive them. If we are truly sorry, God will receive us. Take a moment and ponder then, that if we could earn our salvation by doing good deeds, why did Jesus come to die in our place? God knows that we are all sinners and still loved us. He died for us while we were yet sinners. The Bible tells us so in the following verse:

"But God commendeth his love toward us, in that, while we were yet sinners, Christ died for us."
Romans 5:8 King James Version (KJV)

God also says in his word that if we have broken one of the commandments we have broken them all. Proving that nobody can keep them, they were provided to be a guide.

> *"For whosoever shall keep the whole law, and yet offend in one point, he is guilty of all."*
> *James 2:10 King James Version (KJV)*

The Bible says the law is our schoolmaster in the following verse:

> *"Wherefore, the law, was our schoolmaster to bring us unto Christ, that we might be justified by faith. But after that faith is come, we are no longer under a schoolmaster. For ye are all the children of God by faith in Christ Jesus."*
> *Galatians 3:24-26 King James Version (KJV)*

It is our belief in Jesus that saves us, not our works. Only one human being on earth could keep all of the commandments, and that was Jesus. No other human being on earth has never sinned. We are all sinners, as the Bible tells us:

> *"As it is written, There is none righteous, no, not one."*
> *Romans 3:10 King James Version (KJV)*

If we struggle with a certain sin, God just wants us to ask him to help us overcome that sin so that we can have a closer walk with him. He will help you. Do not deny the sin you may be doing; instead ask Jesus Christ to help you overcome it. He already knows what we are doing, so we are not deceiving him, only ourselves. The Bible says that God is not willing that any should perish.

> *"The Lord is not slack concerning his promise, as some men count slackness; but is longsuffering to us-ward, not willing that any should perish, but that all should come to repentance."*
> *2 Peter 3:9 King James Version (KJV)*

~

> *"Have I any pleasure at all that the wicked should die? saith the Lord God: and not that he should return from his ways, and live?"*
> Ezekiel 18:23 King James Version (KJV)

Some believe Jesus is not protecting his people, pointing out that so many of them are persecuted and martyred. The verse above says he waits patiently so that more people can get saved before he returns to judge. His goodness —not his weakness— causes him to hold on. That's because he has no weaknesses.

In the following chapter, we will read the supernatural proof that the Bible was in fact given to us from God to help us walk through life here on earth, that it is in fact the Holy Word of God, and that no man on earth has the authority to change it.

Chapter 3:

God's Authority on Earth

"For the word of God is quick, and powerful, and sharper than any two-edged sword, piercing even to the dividing asunder of soul and spirit, and of the joints and marrow, and is a discerner of the thoughts and intents of the heart."
Hebrews 4:12 King James Version (KJV)

THE BEST WAY to get to know God and to begin to hear from him is to read his word. God's adversary and our adversary has been very busy trying to keep this supernatural book from getting into our hands throughout the centuries. This tells us that whatever it says inside must be very valuable, or they would not try to keep it hidden from us. In this chapter, I go into detail as to who the adversary is and back it up with a timeline of history that is provable.

The best evidence regarding the truth of the Bible comes directly from the actions of God's adversaries since Jesus' resurrection. I'll walk us through a Biblical timeline of who it was in history who murdered millions of Jesus' followers, just for reading the Bible and trying to pass it along for others to read. Then I will show you why the King James Version of the Bible is the only one we should read.

God's adversary has tried to alter God's Word, burn it, claim ownership of it, and keep it hidden from people for centuries. He apparently did not succeed in any of his attempts because we still have God's word today, and it is translated into more than five hundred languages and counting. It is indestructible and has stood the test of time. Many, who do not know the power of God, need more evidence.

If the adversary did not know that the information the Bible contains could set humanity free from him, then he would not have exerted such efforts throughout history to try to remove it from the world. No other book in history has been at the center of so much bloodshed as the Holy Scriptures, not because of God but because of the devil not wanting us to get our hands on it. The devil knows that if he can kill people in the name of Jesus, then people will not wish to turn to Jesus for salvation. It is what God's adversaries have done for centuries.

Jesus wants us to know that the murder committed throughout the centuries in his name—for example, the Spanish Inquisition and the Holocaust—were not and are not commanded by him. He had no part in these horrendous actions led by the Papacy.

The adversary did these acts in the name of Jesus so that people would hate Jesus. Many people do not believe in Jesus because of the acts of violence from the adversary in history claiming to be the church of Jesus Christ.

The adversary has done an excellent job; I have to say. It has worked for centuries. All the while, he sits back and laughs at humanity and how it has fallen into all the traps he has laid out for us. Jesus wants us to know that he is the good God and that he would never order the massacre of his loyal followers.

Jesus himself is the head of his church. Jesus rose from the dead, is sitting at the right hand of his Father, and is King over his church. We do not need a human intercessor; Jesus intercedes for us. His Spirit lives in all of his people and the Bible is his word. If we want to know Jesus better, we can just read his word. Being born again means that Jesus' Spirit comes to dwell inside of us. His Spirit leads us and directs us each individually and each person is part of his church; we are not inside of a building per se.

Jesus would never order the massacre of anyone, he is a loving God and he would never kill his own followers. I placed the definition of a heretic according to the Catholic Church. The following is from the Catholic Encyclopedia, pg. 368:

> *"In the code of canon law the term heretic means a baptized person, who, while retaining the name of Christian, stubbornly denies or calls in doubt any truth which is to be accepted on Divine and Catholic Faith. All heretics incur ipso facto excommunication specially reserved in the internal forum to the Holy See; furthermore, unless they repent after being admonished, they are to be deprived of any ecclesiastical benefices, dignities, pensions or offices they have; they are to be declared tainted with infamy, and if they be clerics, after a further fruitless warning they are to be degraded. Again, a similar excommunication is uncurred by those who publish books written by heretics upholding and commending heresy, and by all who defend or knowingly and without due permission read or keep these or any other books prohibited by name by letters Apostolic."*

Thousands died for their faith in Jesus, while others went back to the Catholic Church. It is for this reason the Bible tells us in Revelation that the "Great whore is drunk with the blood of the saints." The Spanish Inquisiton is still in effect today by the way, it was never retracted.

The slaughter in the Inquisition was done by the Papacy. Their main purpose was to keep followers of Jesus from getting the written word of God. Whenever an institution goes to such lengths to hide something from the public, it is a great indication that there is some pretty valuable information in it. Why eles would our adversary, the devil and his church exert such extreme efforts in keeping it hidden from us. God does have enemies, as we can see below, and so do you. Identifying your enemy is the first steps in any battle:

> "Thou shalt not bow down thyself to them, nor serve them: for I, the LORD thy God am a jealous God, **visiting the iniquity of the fathers upon the children unto the third and fourth generation of them that hate me;"**
> Exodus 20:5 King James Version (KJV)

The verse above is clearly speaking about the worship of idols. He goes on to say that these are those that hate him. The Papacy does not hide what they are doing; they do it in the open for all to see. Sadly, this fact will make it harder for each individual on judgment day when they will meet face to face with their Creator Jesus Christ. Satan is our accuser, so he will say: "I did it right in front of their eyes, and they still did not see it." If we have not asked Jesus into our heart already, to have him defend us on that day when the devil accuses us, what will you say?

Do not allow yourself to be stuck in the above mentioned scenario. Let us read our Bible's and find out the truth on our own. I recommend the King James Version because it has been around for over 600 years and is God's approved version. There are other versions, however the one God did not allow the devil to tamper with is the King James Version.

One scholar by the name of David W. Daniels wrote several books about which Bible we should use. *Answers to Your Bible Version Questions* and *Look What's Missing* are two of them. In his book *Answers to Your Bible Version Questions*, he states the following:

> *"The Old Latin Bible was known as the 'Vulgate,' which means 'common Bible.' Once again, God's words were spreading, and many Europeans began translating these Old Latin scriptures into their own languages. The devil responded by preparing a counterfeit 'Vulgate' in Rome. By the 300's, the Roman religion claimed to be true Christianity, and a new 'Bible' was made from the perverted Alexandrian writings. It included the Apocryphal books that the early church had rejected."*

Consequently, whoever did not read Rome's Bible was on Rome's hit list. This is what led to the Spanish Inquisition. Any individual not pledging allegiance to the Catholic Church were termed heretics, even followers of Jesus. Bible believers attempting to uphold the true word were called heretics and were brutally killed by the Roman Empire through the Spanish Inquisition.

The apocrypha are additional books that were not approved by the Jewish scholars, but the Catholic Church added them to the Bible anyways. In Mr. Daniels book *Look What's Missing* he notes several hundred verses that have been removed from certain Bibles for no apparent reason.

On the following page, I provide just a few of the examples he provides in his book. I highly recommend reading it and researching his claim.

Here are a few examples from Mr. Daniels's book:

"And Phillip said, if thou believest with all thine heart, thou mayest. And he answered and said, I believe that Jesus Christ is the Son of God." *Acts 8:37 KJV*	*Not in the NIV, Message, NLT, ESV, NET, NRS, or twenty-nine other Bibles.*
"For the Son of man is come to save that which is lost." *Matthew 18:11 KJV*	*Missing from the NIV, TNIV, RSV, ERV (Westcott & Hort) and twenty-two other Bibles.*
"And the scripture was fulfilled, which saith, And he was numbered with the transgressors." *Mark 15:28 KJV*	*Not in the NIV, ESV, NRS, NET, NLT, NAB (Catholic) or twenty-one other Bibles.*

The Bible is clear that God's word cannot be changed:

"But the word of the Lord endureth for ever. And this is the word which by the gospel is preached unto you."
1 Peter 1:25 King James Version (KJV)

~

"Heaven and earth will pass away, but my words shall not pass away."
Matthew 24:35 King James Version (KJV)

~

"All scripture is given by inspiration of God, and is profitable for doctrine, for reproof, for correction, for instruction in righteousness."
2 Timothy 3:16 King James Version (KJV)

The Lord Jesus is not in agreement with the teachings of the Roman Empire and is not a part of it in any way, it is not his church. The Pope calls himself the 'Holy Father' when the Bible says there is only one Holy Father, and we are not to call anyone else Father on earth.

> "And **call no man** your father upon the earth: for one is your Father, which is in heaven."
> Matthew 23:9 King James Version (KJV)

Jesus identifies the counterfeit church and even calls her a harlot, due to her idolatry in Revelation 17:5 King James Version(KJV):

> "And upon her forehead was a name written, MYSTERY, BABYLON THE GREAT, THE MOTHER OF HARLOTS AND ABOMINATIONS OF THE EARTH."

'Mystery' Babylon is clearly identified through the connection between Roman Catholicism and Voodoo in chapter five as the Voodoo gods are also called 'Mysteries.' The Roman Catholic System places their theology and philosophy above the Holy Scriptures—The Word of God—and is still ensuing today.

God's Word says not to believe men's philosophies:

> "Beware lest any man spoil you through philosophy and vain deceit, after the tradition of men, after the rudiments of the world, and not after Christ."
> Colossians 2:8 King James Version (KJV)

Not only is the Bible the best-selling book of all time, but there are also more than 2,000 prophecies or predictions of future events that God placed in there to guide his people throughout the centuries. More evidence that the Holy Scriptures are, in fact, from God, was displayed through the prophecies. No other book has this claim because The Bible is, in fact, the Word of God. It is a supernatural book, by a supernatural God who used faithful men of God to write it.

What Other Proof of the Bible's Validity Exists?
There is a lot of evidence that the Holy Scriptures came from God. Of more than 2,000 prophecies or predictions that God wrote in the Holy Scriptures, more than half have already taken place.

Seven Testimonies that the Bible is the Truth

1. The Testimony of Internal Consistency - The Bible is a codex of books put together and divided into two testaments. It was written over 1,500 years, by more than 40 authors, on three continents. All had various backgrounds, living during different periods in different places, and all writing about one of the most controversial topics in the world—God. All these men in various situations wrote about the same thing with no contradiction. This alone is valid proof; it was the Holy Ghost of God.
2. The Testimony of His Truth - History confirms the authenticity of the Bible with fulfilled predictions.
3. The Testimony of Archeology - The finding of the Dead Sea Scrolls from 1946 to 1956 confirms the Bible's accuracy. These ancient manuscripts date back to 70 A.D., according to the archeologists who discovered them.
4. The Testimony of Science - Science testifies to the power of God. "It is He that sitteth upon the circle of the earth.." Isaiah 40:22 - Here we see that the Bible told us the earth was round before scientists discovered this fact. "... and hangeth the earth upon nothing." Job 26:7 - The Bible told us the Earth floats freely in the universe before scientists discovered this fact.
5. The Testimony of Relevance - The Bible was written 2,000 years ago and still gives answers to today's problems. It is

still the best-selling book of all time, with more than 26 billion copies sold of the King James Version alone. Only God could be behind these numbers.

6. The Testimony of a Changed Life - No other book can strengthen the intellect and change people's lives like the Bible. A person's changed life authenticates the validity of the Bible.
7. The Testimony of Prophecy - Fulfilled Bible prophecy proves the truthfulness of God's word and gives us confidence that the future is in his hands. More than half of the Bible's 2,000 predictions have already taken place.

Only God knows the future. He is the only one who could have given the prophecies contained in the scriptures and—more importantly—fulfilled them all. More than 1,800 and counting have been fulfilled to date.

Who Wrote the Bible?

There are two answers to the question of who wrote the Bible. As a divine document, its words ultimately come from God who chose holy men, selected by Him to write it. It tells us that the Bible is God-breathed in 2 Timothy 3:15 King James Version (KJV):

"All scripture is given by inspiration of God, and is profitable for doctrine, for reproof, for correction, for instruction in righteousness:"

"Knowing this first, that no prophecy of the scripture is of any private interpretation. For the prophecy came not in old time by the will of man: but holy men of God spake as they were moved by the Holy Ghost."
2 Peter 1:20-21 King James Version (KJV)

God directed the human authors of the Bible, using their writing styles and personalities to produce the words of his choosing. The human authors involved included approximately 40 writers with diverse backgrounds and from diverse locations, over the course of 1,500 years. Isaiah was a prophet, Ezra was a priest, Matthew was a tax collector, John was a fisherman, Moses was a shepherd, and Luke was a physician.

The authors each present different perspectives, yet they all proclaim the same God and the same singular path of salvation—Jesus (John 3:16 KJV; 14:6 KJV; Acts 4:12 KJV).

Listed on the following two pages are the books, the names of their authors and the approximate dates of their writing.

OLD COVENANT

Book	Writer	Time Period
Genesis, Exodus, Leviticus, Numbers, Deuteronomy	Moses	1440-1400 B.C.
Joshua	Joshua	1350 B.C.
Judges, Ruth, 1 & 2 Samuel	Samuel, Nathan, Gad	1000-900 B.C.
1&2 Kings	Jeremiah	600 B.C.
1&2 Chronicles, Ezra, Nehemiah	Ezra	450 B.C.
Esther	Mordecai	400 B.C.
Job	Possibly Moses – not certain	1400 B.C. Date uncertain
Psalm	Half by King David others written by Moses	400 B.C. to 1400 B.C.
Proverbs, Ecclesiastes, Song of Solomon	Solomon	900 B.C.
Isaiah	Isaiah	700 B.C.
Jeremiah, Lamentations	Jeremiah	600 B.C.
Ezekiel	Ezekiel	550 B.C.
Daniel	Daniel	550 B.C.
Hosea	Hosea	750 B.C.
Joel	Joel	850 B.C.
Amos	Amos	750 B.C.
Obadiah	Obadiah	600 B.C.
Jonah	Jonah	700 B.C.
Micah	Micah	700 B.C.
Nahum	Nahum	650 B.C.
Habakkuk	Habakkuk	600 B.C.
Zephaniah	Zephaniah	650 B.C.
Haggai	Haggai	520 B.C.
Zechariah	Zechariah	500 B.C.
Malachi	Malachi	430 B.C.

Jeremiah 31:31 King James Version (KJV)
"Behold, the days come, saith the Lord, that I will make a new covenant with the house of Israel, and with the house of Judah:"

Once we become a believer in Jesus Christ, we are grafted in with his people the Israelites in Romans 11:11-23.

NEW COVENANT

BOOK	WRITER	TIME PERIOD
Matthew	Matthew	55-70 A.D.
Mark	John Mark	50-65 A.D.
Luke	Luke	60-65 A.D.
John	John	90 A.D.
Acts	Luke	60-65 A.D.
Romans 1 Corinthians 2 Corinthians Galatians Ephesians Philippians Colossians 1 Thessalonians 2 Thessalonians 1 Timothy 2 Timothy Titus Philemon	Paul	50-67 A.D.
Hebrews	Unknown	60 A.D.
James	James	45-50 A.D.
1 Peter 2 Peter	Peter	60 A.D.
Jude	Jude	60 A.D.
Revelation	John	90-96 A.D.

Why Do People Refuse To Believe That The Bible Is God's Word?

One of the most important questions of all time is: "Is the Bible really from God?" If the Bible is the Word of God, it changes everything—the way we view life, the way we live life, and the choices we make. Failures to follow, obey, and trust it will have eternal consequences. To ignore God's word is to ignore our Maker, so adhesion to it should be crucial to our loved ones and us.

The Bible is also one of the ways that God shows us his love. God did not have to communicate anything to humanity, but he chose to so that we could know him, enjoy fellowship with him, and understand the world and ourselves. If God had not taken the first step in revealing himself to us through his word, we would not know him.

We would be left to deduce what we could about the world from what we could sense. However, our Creator has graciously shown us the truth, and it is in the Bible. God is our creator (Isaiah 40:28 KJV), he is our authority (Isaiah 43:15 KJV), and his word is the final authority for the human race. It is the only entirely trustworthy moral litmus test (1 John 2:5 KJV). It explains life and death and gives us a clear understanding of right and wrong.

How, then, do we know for sure that the Bible we have is the actual word of God? Can the Bible possibly be just another 'holy book'? What is the evidence that the Bible we buy in the bookstore today is truly the word of God? The Bible says it is the word of God in 2 Timothy 3:16 King James Version (KJV).

> *"All Scripture is given by inspiration of God and is profitable for doctrine, for reproof, for correction, for instruction in righteousness:"*

This verse is an example of an 'internal' piece of evidence that the Bible is the word of God and that we should only purchase the King James Version because it has not been corrupted.

Internal evidence is made up of those statements in the Bible that claim its divine origin. A few other pieces of internal evidence include the unity of the Bible, its fulfilled prophecies, and the unique, powerful authority people have found within its pages throughout history. In addition to this, Jesus is the person to be raised from the dead. No other prophet can make this claim in any other religion known to mankind.

The unity of the Bible means that, even though it was written by many authors over three continents and in three languages, it is cohesive down to the last detail. There are no mistakes; it all works together perfectly. It is truly a miracle.

The fulfilled prophecies in the Bible also indicate that it is God's word. Hundreds of prophecies about future kingdoms and nations and the Messiah were put forth and then fulfilled, sometimes hundreds of years later. Unlike many modern prophecies, the prophecies in the scriptures are met down to the last detail as explained in the book Exploring Bible Prophecy by LaHaye, Tim F., and Edward E. Hindson. Statistically, there is no way this happened by chance; the only explanation is that the Bible is of divine origin.

The Bible's unique authority and power are another piece of internal evidence for its divine origin. The millions of changed lives reveal its power throughout human history. Martyrs have given up their lives to preserve its truth. Sinners throughout the ages have been convicted and changed by it.

Broken hearts are healed by God's comforting voice emanating from its pages, and salvation has been graciously made available through its record of the life and sacrifice of Jesus. No other book in human history has such power to change lives as the Bible does; it is truly the word of the God who created life. It does not contain any lies, and, therefore, carries a spiritual light within it. Thus, when we read the Bible, our life—whether we realize it or not—changes little by little.

Besides these instances of internal evidence, there is external evidence that the Bible is God's word: The Bible's historicity, the integrity of its human authors, and its indestructibility.

The phrase 'historicity of the Bible' refers to the fact that it corresponds accurately to descriptions of historical events recorded by non-religious sources. Archeological events and historical writings prove the Bible to be true such as in the book The Case for Jesus written by Brant Pitre. This is a well-documented source of information about the ancient world. The accurate historical records found in the Bible give us proof of the similar truthfulness in its discussion of spiritual subjects.

The integrity of its human authors is another piece of the external evidence of the Bible's accuracy. When the lives of the authors of Scripture are studied, we find that they were honest men. Their willingness to die for what they believed in proves that they were sure of the truth of their testimonies. Those who wrote the New Testament (as well as five hundred other eyewitnesses) had seen Jesus after he rose from the dead. If they had been lying about seeing him, at least one of them would have admitted as such in the face of persecution. Why would so many of them suffer and die for a message they knew to be false?

All the Apostles, without exception, remained faithful to their testimonies until the end of their lives (1 Corinthians 15:6 KJV). Peter was scared to the point that he denied knowing Jesus three times, prior to seeing him raised from the dead. It was not until he saw Jesus risen from the dead that Peter gained the strength to do the work God called him to do. We can read about it in Luke 24:33-37 KJV.

Paul also states in 1 Corinthians 15:3-7 KJV that Jesus was seen by five hundred other people all at one time as he says in 1 Corinthians 15:3-7 King James Version (KJV):

"For I delivered unto you first of all that which I also received, how that Christ died for our sins according to the scriptures; And that he was buried, and that he rose again the third day according to the scriptures: And that he was seen of Cephas, then of the twelve: After that, he was seen of above five hundred brethren at once; of whom the greater part remain unto this present, but some are fallen asleep. After that, he was seen of James; then of all the apostles."

When we have a witness in a court proceeding, doesn't it make our case more believable? Jesus had 500 eyewitnesses; our courts require only two for credibility purposes. It is for this reason that we know Jesus is real.

Finally, the indestructibility of the Bible is strong evidence that it is God's word. The Bible, in contrast to the books of every other religion, humbles man, suggests man's inability to save himself and demonstrates the need for God's grace instead (Ephesians 2:8-9 KJV). Because of its 'offensive' message, the Bible has endured more attacks and attempts at destruction than any other book in history. The first attack was done by the early Roman leaders, then by the communist dictators, then by the atheists and agnostics of modern and postmodern times.

The Bible has survived and is still published more than any other book worldwide with numbers above six billion copies sold. Only God himself could be behind such numbers. There is no other book in history that has sold more copies than the Bible — more proof of this wonderful supernatural book.

Throughout the ages, skeptics have called the Bible a myth, but archeological records have proven its historicity. Others have denounced its teachings as outdated and useless, but its positive impact on the moral and legal systems of cultures around the world is undeniable.

Scientists, psychologists, and politicians continue to attack the Bible, but its truth has never been disproven, and its light has never been snuffed out. It continues to change lives and cultures, just as it did 2,000 years ago. God supernaturally protects the Bible, proving that it is his word, just as it claims to be.

Bible Versions

Most of the translations we use today have important verses removed purposely by the Jesuits – the secret army of the Vatican as detailed in Author David Daniels book *Look What's Missing*. As we may already know, in any battle the goal is to divide and conquer. The adversary has done and is doing just that to Christian churches today. He keeps many pastors busy in churches by influencing them so much that they stay focused on spiritual gifts of healing, raising the dead, and signs and wonders and not on the Word of God. The Word of God is where the power is, and the devil knows this. That is why he has infiltrated the other versions and has removed verses and changed words.

God did work in signs and wonders back then because he was witnessing to Jews who required a sign for them to believe. We must remember that in those days they did not have a Bible. All they knew were the five books of Moses. Therefore, God had to work with signs and wonders. The Apostles laid the foundation of the church and have always to this date been separate from the Catholic Church; they did not come out of the reformation because they were never part of it.

Today, God's power is displayed through his word. In the following chapter, I will show you why I believe we should honor Jesus in truth during Passover.

Chapter 4:

King Jesus, Not the Easter Bunny

"Jesus saith unto her, Mary. She turned herself, and saith unto him, Rabboni; which is to say, Master.
Jesus saith unto her, Touch me not; for I am not yet ascended to my Father: but go to my brethren, and say unto them, I ascend unto my Father, and your Father; and to my God, and your God.
Mary Magdalene came and told the disciples that she had seen the Lord, and that He had spoken these things unto her."
John 20:16-18 King James Version (KJV)

JESUS'S BODY WAS heavily guarded by Roman soldiers when they placed him behind the stone to make sure nobody could take away his body after he died.

When Mary arrived at the site, she saw Jesus in his resurrected body and said "Rabbi" in complete astonishment. The resurrection of Jesus was so supernatural and miraculous that they had no choice but to believe that Jesus was the Messiah because they saw him die, then they saw him alive again.

Jesus raised the dead during his ministry, and then God raised him from the dead after three days. As we can see, God is very real. He surprises us because humans live in the natural world; our thoughts are in the physical realm. When something so supernatural happens, we have no choice but to believe that it is a work only God could do. God is so real, alive, and active in our daily lives.

In today's age, we can fly to Jerusalem and see where Jesus walked, preached, and lived. We can also see his people the Israelites and Christians persecuted daily as another form of proof that the Bible is real.

> *"Yea, and all that will live godly in Christ Jesus shall suffer persecution."*
> *2 Timothy 3:12 King James Version (KJV)*

For most believers, the resurrection is not even real. Why? Because of the way, we have been celebrating Passover! We are to be witnesses first to the Jews. Associating the Passover with bunny rabbits and Easter eggs leads many Jewish people not to understand or believe in Jesus. Our witness to the Jews is a great responsibility. The Bible says we are to be a witness to his people first in Romans 1:16 King James Version (KJV):

"For I am not ashamed of the gospel of Christ: for it is the power of God unto salvation to every one that believeth; **to the Jew first***, and also* **to the Greek***."*

The power of the resurrection should touch our weaknesses and our entire lives. We should see evidence of this in our lives, and others should see our light as well.

We must be born again; our lives should have changed. They should break strongholds and all the vices the enemy has placed as obstacles before us. Jesus and his resurrection were the first fruits, meaning that whatever happened in that tomb is the beginning and not the end. It was the first of what should come afterward. We should see miracles happening in our church every day, not people dying of cancer and infirmities that the Messiah has power over! The celebration of Passover should be a continuous celebration all year long of his supernatural resurrection.

We are here because Jesus rose from the grave and overcame life and death. He rose from the dead so that we could rise from all of our problems and have victory in our life. He did not rise so that we could go Easter egg hunting or paint some eggs.

I do not recall Peter the Apostle or Mary going off to paint Easter eggs after witnessing Jesus's resurrection. Let us no longer fall for the devil's schemes. Jesus is the Passover lamb so that we can be renewed and live a victorious life in him. He rose so that we can overcome evil, as well as all of our fears and physical ailments.

Worship in Truth to Gain Our Freedom

Most people, including Christians, are celebrating a pagan rite in their hearts, and we are all guilty of this. Turning the Passover celebration into a fairytale diminishes its power in our lives. Jesus's resurrection was the first fruit, which means there are better things that follow the resurrection. This miracle was just the beginning or the first of what is yet to come.

Freedom is what Passover and Days of Unleavened Bread are memorializing. The Israelites celebrate because they were set free from the bondage of Egypt. Believers should celebrate Passover because it represents freedom from paying for our sins and not going to hell.

Leaven has always represented sin in the Bible, so during this time we need to remove anything that causes us to sin, remove the leaven from our lives, and focus on that. It is a period of examination of where we stand in Christ. It is a time of change and a time to allow God to work in our lives after we turn from sin—a spiritual check-up if you will. Paul told us to examine ourselves in 2 Corinthians 13:5 King James Version (KJV):

"Examine yourselves, whether ye be in the faith; prove your own selves. Know ye not your own selves, how that Jesus Christ is in you, except ye be reprobates?"

Truth and freedom go together; once we worship in truth, we have freedom. The majority of the entire Christian world is being lulled by Satan who orchestrated all these pagan holidays using the Catholic Church to do so. In falling for Satan's schemes, the resurrection of Jesus is not celebrated in the manner that God commands us to. We cannot mix true and false worship; God hates it. The book of Ezekiel is almost entirely all the wrath of God upon the Israelites due to the mixture of pagan idol worship and true worship. We are aware that Christ died for our sins, but miss the full impact of that fact because we do not observe the Passover—hence the lesson and power is lost.

True worship will produce the freedom we lack in our churches, our finances, our families, and our countries. We can know something is real and true, but if we fail to use it, what good is it? It is worthless unless it is used. Freedom and truth come to those who press on; it occurs progressively and not all at once.

CHAPTER 4: KING JESUS, NOT THE EASTER BUNNY

These are lessons from the Days of Unleavened Bread. The Israelites took seven days to get to and cross the Red Sea, and then it took them another 40 years to get into their land, their inheritance—the Promised Land.

There was a time when their journey began, but if they had never continued, they would never have had their land, their inheritance, or their freedom. We must continue to press on in truth. If we remain in truth, then we will truly be disciples. We will understand the truth, and we will become free.

Our children need to know that Jesus rose from the dead, and our days should be filled with nothing but celebrations, focusing on the resurrection power of Jesus, instead of on eggs and cute little bunnies. Let us stop taking something so supernatural like Jesus' resurrection and turning our minds to something representing the natural realm by substituting it with eggs and bunny rabbits.

Imagine the power we would have in our services and prayers if we gave true worship to Jesus Christ. It does not matter how many times we sanctify it, practicing these rituals only keeps us from the truth and freedom of his resurrection. We must focus on turning people from sin. The Scriptures say that by doing this, we cover many of our own sins in James 5:20 King James Version (KJV).

"Let him know, that he which converteth the sinner from the error of his way shall save a soul from death, and shall hide a multitude of sins."

If the Jews celebrated Passover for seven days in commemoration of being delivered from the Egyptians, how much more should we celebrate who have inherited eternal salvation and freedom from hell? Undoubtedly much longer than a week, don't you agree? There are Asians who celebrate their gods and pagan traditions far longer than this—some lasting longer than a week. Businesses close all over China in honor of their pagan gods, and we do not do the same for our Savior, who suffered such a horrible death for us. It is because of our lack of teaching the truth about our Passover Lamb in our churches that our country is in its current state. Catholic customs reach into even our most fundamental churches today through Easter, Christmas, St. Valentine's Day, St. Patrick's Day, and Halloween.

Passover should be our biggest celebration of the entire year. It needs to be ingrained into the very hearts and minds of our children and our children's children. It should not be a 'one day, one hour of the week' celebration.

We are going to heaven, we are saved and delivered from the powers of darkness. We walk in the supernatural, not the natural, we are healed, we are delivered, and we are free. Might our actions coincide with our decree of being delivered and set free. A week sabbatical in which businesses close down in honor of our risen Savior. Let us fellowship with our brothers and sisters in Christ and repent of our sins.

We need to prepare for the coming of the Lord, and honoring him in truth would be a good start. Heaven will be a celebration of the resurrection and the breaking of bondage for eternity. I believe we must prepare for this type of holiday starting now.

Where Did Easter Originate?

The myth of Easter is not even a provable story. Easter is not found anywhere in history. What is the origin of Easter? Since the sun rises in the east, the pagans titled their holiday as Easter. Sun worshipers worship the sun that rises in the east, the root word for Easter. Witches today still position their beds facing east to honor the rising sun. Satan ties most holidays to nature, so we don't seek God and is used as a misdirection tactic.

CHAPTER 4: KING JESUS, NOT THE EASTER BUNNY

Tying everything to nature as most witchcraft does, Easter has us focusing on eggs and rabbits, instead of Jesus. It has turned the resurrection of Jesus—something so miraculous and supernatural—into a fable and tied it to nature through bunny rabbits and eggs.

Pagan celebrations are because it is all a fable. They are beautiful stories, but none are real! There is no evidence in history of their claims. They are based on the natural realm, venerating things such as mother earth and Mother Nature, and they remove God from the equation. They base their belief on cycles and have no real connection to life or a changing reborn life that the resurrection offers.

The coloring of eggs goes back to sun worship and the Druids, who used to color their eggs scarlet in honor of the sun. They would leave dyed eggs on tombs for the rebirth of their loved ones. Dyeing eggs for ritual purposes goes back to the Egyptians, who did it for purposes of fertility rites, chanting, bon-fires, and leaping through flames. All of these are still practiced today in Voodoo and Santeria. An initiate into this religion has to pass through the fire—they literally walk through fire.

Let us no longer water down the gospel by celebrating Easter; it has de-radicalized the resurrection, disconnected the supernatural, and connected us to the natural world. It is so easy to get comfortable with this way of life, and then it becomes a ritual. The profound gospel of Jesus Christ changes lives. In placing the Easter Bunny and eggs before Jesus, they severed the reality of his resurrection and removed it from its Jewish roots. When we dilute it with fables, the resurrection loses all power. It is another sleight of hand, created by the mixing of truth with lies.

Jesus is real; He died a real, excruciating death at the hands of real Roman soldiers. Faithful disciples saw him die and saw him rise again. He still does miracles today!

Who Changed the Date of Passover?
It is best to note first off, that the Apostles never observed Easter as we call it, it is very clear throughout the Bible that they observed Passover (God's) festival. The Apostle Paul confirms that he kept the customary observance of Passover, as was given him by Christ himself, when he said in 1 Corinthians 11:23 King James Version (KJV):

"For I received of the Lord that which also I delivered unto you, that the Lord Jesus the same night in which he was betrayed took bread:"

With this information established, how then was it changed from the 14th of Nisan to the Sunday following the first full moon after the vernal equinox, and assigned the pagan name Easter? This is no minor change from the original Passover date exemplified by Jesus himself. The authority of Jesus is superseded when this is changed and is considered a heretical act.

At the Council of Nicaea, they set the day of Easter to link with the vernal equinox and called it a holy day. They labeled anyone who did celebrate it on the actual Passover timeframe - which is the 14th day of Nisan in the Jewish calendar—the '14ers'. Ultimately, all the Jewish celebrations were removed and replaced with pagan days that honored natural dates to worship the sun and the moon. (Catholic Encyclopedia, pg. 228)

Here is the quote from the Catholic Encyclopedia stating they have no need to keep the Jewish holiday:

"...the question thus debated was therefore primarily whether Easter was to be kept on a Sunday, or whether Christians should observe the Holy Day of the Jews, the fourteen of Nisan which might occur on any day of the week."

Here is another stating they excommunicated those who did keep the Jewish Passover of the 14th of Nissan (Catholic Encyclopedia pg. 225):

> *"Those who continued to keep Easter with the Jews were called Quartodecimens (14 Nisan) and were excluded from the church."*

The 14ers were people who celebrated Passover on the 14th of Nisan, which meant they celebrated the Passover Lamb correctly from the Jewish culture just as the Jews do today. The devil does not care how far away we are from God's commandments we are, just as long as we break them. If he can create a date different from God's commanded time and get us to worship on that day instead of the actual date, then he just got us to sin. Not only has he caused us to sin, but anyone whom we teach the same we are causing them to sin as well. I believe that as followers of Jesus, we must worship on his commanded time for Passover and not on the man-made date of Easter. It is called Easter because the sun comes up in the East, and they worship the sun. When we worship at this time of year, we are honoring their god the sun, or Easter. We cannot mix worship or we will no longer be worshiping in Spirit and in truth as God commands.

It is clear that anything the Catholic Church changes may have an underlying blessing for us as believers in Jesus or they would not change it to begin with.

Next, I will reveal another way the adversary masks his deception and what it means for you and I.

Chapter 5:

The Mask of Deception

*"Thou shalt have no other gods before me.
Thou shalt not make unto thee any graven image, or any likeness of any thing that is in heaven above, or that is in the earth beneath, or that is in the water under the earth.
Thou shalt not bow down thyself to them, nor serve them: for I the Lord thy God am a jealous God, visiting the iniquity of the fathers upon the children unto the third and fourth generation of them that hate me;"
Exodus 20:2-5 King James Version (KJV)*

On August 27, 2015, I started thinking about where the Catholics were in Biblical times so that I could provide further understanding. Knowing that Catholicism is a mask for Voodoo, I went on Google to research Benin, Africa—the place of origin of Voodoo and Santeria—to see if I could find some more information there.

Benin used to be called Dahomey (Dan's home from the tribe of Dan). As I scrolled down, I saw an image that looked like a man with a shark head in place of his head. The King of Dahomey was Behanzin, who was the eleventh ruler of this kingdom. The shark head was a symbol of his reign. Many Believers place this fish symbol on their vehicles thinking it is of Christian origin. The hat the Popes sometimes wear is symbolic of the shark head that looks like a fish as well. The Etymology of the city of Nineveh is such that the Babylonian Nina was a place where fish were very abundant, and Ishtar or Nina, the goddess of the city, was associated with Ninmah, as goddess of reproduction. The date of this foundation is unknown, but it may have taken place approximately in 3,000 B.C.

In the seventeenth century, the Fon tribe conquered the lands of the current chief at that time, whose name was 'Dan,' in Benin. This led to the name Dan-Home or Dahomey, which means 'in the belly of Dan, because it is in the town of Abomey, where the remains of Dan are buried, according to the Fon people. In reading the entire page, I scrolled down to the bottom to an external link to the Museum Theme of the Kingdom of Dahomey. As the web page pulled up, I clicked on the link that said 'Vodun' and continued reading about the name of their god and how they worship the god Dangbe.

It read:

"Worship of the Serpent god Dan or Dangbe, whose ancestors are the python, is particularly prevalent in Ouida as it was in the ancient kingdom of Xweda."

The serpent god in Voodoo is named Danballa, and as we may already know, when a serpent slithers, he always leaves a trail.

This information gives light to a completely new outlook on Voodoo, Catholicism, and Islam— showing them as being all one in the same. They all worship the same god, the serpent god <u>Dan</u> <u>Baal</u> <u>Allah</u>, in Voodoo spelled Danballah. Danballah's symbol is a serpent made with the colors of the rainbow. We can see who is behind the gay movement in America from this. It is the serpent spirit Danballah from Voodoo. When we pray, we must pray the Lord rebuke Danballah out of this country.

To prove Danballah's association with Catholocism, let's explore the connections between Dan, Voodoo, and the Catholic Church. Dan is from the lost tribe of Israel, which is the only tribe not sealed in the book of Revelation. Bal is a derivative of the word 'Ba'al' in Hebrew and means 'possessor' or 'lord over,' and 'Alla' at the end represents the god of Islam, 'Allah.' Consequently, in Voodoo it is common to allow the loas or their gods to possess followers' bodies, giving these loas or gods total control over their bodies, or possessing them. In Islam, Dawah means the proselytizing or preaching of Islam. Note the prefix Da in their word just as in Voodoo from the tribe of Dan.

I believe that it may be possible that the people in Benin, Africa, today are of the lost tribe of Dan. The tribe of Dan was idolatrous, just like those involved in Voodoo and Catholicism.

The lost tribe of Dan is the only tribe in the book of Revelation that is not sealed. It is believed to be due to their idolatry, as displayed in the following verse:

> "And the children of Dan set up the graven image: and Jonathan, the son of Gershom, the son of Manasseh, he and his sons were priests to the tribe of Dan until the day of the captivity of the land. And they set them up **Micah's** graven image, which he made, all the time that the house of God was in Shiloh."
> Judges 18:30-31 King James Version (KJV)

The religion of Islam requires followers to go to Mecca as part of being a Muslim. Idolatry takes many forms and is a basis of their doctrine in false religions, and Islam is just one of Mama's girls (The Catholic Church being the 'Mother Church' who gave birth to Communism, Nazism, Islam, and Masonry among others).

As we can begin to see, idol worship is an enormous issue with God, and he hates it when people practice idol worshiping. The entire book of Ezekiel is God's wrath on the Israelites for idol worshiping. Jacob, Dan's father, in the following verse foretells Dan's destiny:

> "Dan shall be a serpent by the way, an adder in the path, that biteth the horse heels, so that his rider shall fall backward."
> Genesis 49:17 King James Version (KJV)

I took photographs of the interior of La Ermita de la Caridad, a Catholic Church in Miami, Florida. There is a serpent in a stained glass window in the inner sanctuary. The serpent always leaves a trail, thankfully, and this is how we can trace Catholicism back to the tribe of Dan.

The serpent is known to bite the horses' heels and cause them to fall back and stumble. It is my belief that God did not seal the tribe of Dan in the book of Revelation, along with the other tribes of Israel, due to their idolatry and disobedience.

Throughout history, God used the wicked to bring captivity and judgment upon his people. Similarly, the serpents in the tribe of Dan did the same to God's people and caused many to stumble through idolatry, even to this day. Hence, they were removed from being sealed. As mentioned earlier, the snake slithers and always leaves a trail.

Another god in Voodoo is Legba, which means 'god of the sun' in Fon language. His symbol is the cross because he is the master of the crossroads. He governs all actions of the spirits in Voodoo.

CHAPTER 6: GUILTY BY ASSOCIATION

He controls gates, doors, and entryways; no deity may join a Vodun ceremony unless Legba (Sun god) has been asked to open the gate.

It is suspect that the mark of Dan was found first in Denmark (or Dan mark). The flag of Denmark has a cross with eight lines, just as they have at St. Peter's Basilica in an aerial view. The eight-lined cross is also in many of the portals called 'veves' in Voodoo. It is suspected that this cross may be the mark of Dan and that is the reason it was used as an instrument of torture for Jesus and others who died by crucifixion. We are not to worship the cross.

The tribe of Dan also loved to sail the seas and conquer lands, which is characteristic of what the Catholic Church does to this day. If need be, they will take it by force like they did in the Spanish Inquisition. Therefore, another of their symbols is a sailboat displayed at the Vatican Palace that is also a veve symbol for one of the gods in Voodoo named Agwe. It is the same veve, or drawing made of cornmeal; remember, the serpent always leaves a trail.

Other countries the tribe of Dan had significant influence over in Europe are the United Kingdom, Sweden, Switzerland, Finland, Scotland, Sweden, and Iceland. Prior to the Protestant Reformation, the majority of these countries proclaimed the Catholic faith. Every one of their flags contains the mark of Dan, the eight crosses or 'crux' in Latin. There is also an occult order that calls itself the Rosicrucians, and its symbol or logo is wings with a sun cross in the middle resembling those used in ancient Egyptian times.

Most of the history of the tribe of Dan has been wiped out, and they depended on ancestral worship and oral communication throughout the centuries. What a great way not to leave a trace! Are you beginning to see how cunning the serpent is?

Members of the Fon tribe in Benin, Africa, also plainly state that its dead ancestors have told them that they are from the tribe of Dan. (Musee Ouidah 1992)

Pope John Paul II met with Voodoo priests while in Benin, Africa, in 1993.[3] The Pope told the Voodoo priests that the Catholic Church was open to dialog with other religions and other spiritual families and even atheists so that they can enrich one another. He went on to state that "the II Vatican Council recognized that there are seeds of the word, in the various religious traditions."

Mixing the Bible truth with pagan customs has been customary among the Danites causing many to stumble. The Lembas, who have the Kohen gene, were found in South Africa, and Zimbabwe could be a mixture of the tribe of Dan with the Levite tribe. The following verse tells us how Micah of the tribe of Dan was honored in having a Levitical priest with them because he thought God would do good to him for having him there:

> "And Micah said unto him, Whence comest thou? And he said unto him, I am a Levite of Bethlehemjudah, and I go to sojourn where I may find a place. And Micah said unto him, Dwell with me, and be unto me a father and a priest, and I will give thee ten shekels of silver by the year, and a suit of apparel, and thy victuals. So the Levite went in. And the Levite was content to dwell with the man; and the young man was unto him as one of his sons. And Micah consecrated the Levite; and the young man became his priest, and was in the house of Micah. Then said Micah, Now know I that the LORD will do me good, seeing I have a Levite to my priest."
> Judges 17:9-13 King James Version (KJV)

It is possible that the Levite priest may have mixed with the children of the tribe of Dan and may be the reason the Lembas were found to have the Kohen gene. When I was involved in the

---

[3] As reported by *L'Osservatore Romano*, February 6, 1993, p.4.

occult, the Houngan (Voodoo Priest) told me that many of his clients are of the Judaic religion. According to God's word, Believers are not to associate with or welcome into our homes anyone with any other religious doctrine—if we do; the Bible says we are guilty by association.

Here is the verse:

> *"If there come any unto you, and bring not this doctrine, receive him not into your house, neither bid him God speed: For he that biddeth him God speed is partaker of his evil deeds."*
> *2 John 1:10-13 King James Version (KJV)*

Voodoo practitioners do not believe their religion is from the devil; they believe the lie the devil has told them. They are under his spell. When I was involved with them, I honestly believed it was from God as well, especially because, during their ceremonies, the only object on their altar is Jesus on the cross.

If the adversary is the head of the Voodoo religion, he is also the head of any religions that have stemmed from Voodoo. Whether it was to keep from getting killed in their time or not, because their doctrine is not the same as the word of God that God himself gave us in the Bible, we will be guilty by association by remaining Catholic or in Voodoo or Santeria according to 2 John 1:10-13.

During possession at Voodoo rituals, some humans slither on the floor like serpents; some walk on glass and do not get cut; others float around the peristyle and prophecy to people. God's true servants do not partake in any such acts. I was just a witness when I knew them; I was never involved in any spirit possession, spells or necromancy.

People have died during Voodoo rituals, and this religion is not something anyone should take lightly. Voodoo and the demons and spirits hide in the statues inside a Catholic Church. Each time someone lights a candle in a Catholic Church, they are lighting a candle asking one of these demons to accomplish their requests—they are not the saints of God.

The saints worshiped in Voodoo and Santeria are not even in the Bible. Whether we realize it or not, we are unknowingly worshiping Satan's fallen angels. These are the fallen angels of Satan that he has called out of hell through the veves on the floor during their ceremonies through the middle pole, or 'Poteau Mitan' in Creole.

Santeria is a child religion of Voodoo, and the names of its gods are just slightly different from those of the Voodoo gods, but they are all one and the same. For example, the name of the god of war in Voodoo is Ogun, and in Santeria, it is Ochun. The same saint in Catholicism is called Saint Peter. In all three religions, their followers make shrines to each of their saints and give flower and food offerings to them.

Another one of their goddesses is Yemaya in Santeria, La Siren in Voodoo, and the Black Madonna in Catholicism. Her symbol is the crescent moon. It is the same symbol used in Islam for its god, Allah. Islam is also a child religion of Voodoo and is one of many daughters that the 'Mother Church' has. Nazism, Communism, and Masonry are three more daughters of the 'Mother Church.' The crescent moon is seen under the Black Madonna in the Catholic Church, and I believe it ties Islam and Catholicism together because the serpent always leaves his trail.

There is a book written by a former Catholic priest called Charles Chiniquy. Chiniquy was almost killed several times for converting to Christianity after he could no longer take the strenuous demands of the Papacy. His book is called *50 Years in the Church of Rome*. In this book, he confirms that Voodoo and

Catholicism are one and the same in his chapter about the sun wafer in Catholicism being called 'Bon Dieu'—which is one of the same gods that people of the Voodoo religion worship. He certainly did what the Lord guided him to do in exposing darkness and shining the light on darkness, as stated in the following bible verse in Ephesians 5:11 King James Version (KJV):

"And have no fellowship with the unfruitful works of darkness, but rather reprove them."

Many believe that Voodoo and Catholicism mixed in Haiti and formed a new type of Voodoo, but this is not the case, as the Lord revealed to me that they had to hide their worship to keep from getting killed back in the days of King Saul.

They created underground cities in which they could practice the calling up of the dead and the worshiping of their gods and ancestors without anyone seeing them. Ancestral worship is prominent in Catholicism, Voodoo, and Santeria as well as in Taoism. Egypt was well known for necromancy and preservation of dead bodies, too, just like the Catholic Church does today.

Thousands of Catholic Churches all over the world have cemeteries beneath them. There are churches in Rome where there are entire underground cities. Mystery Babylon in the Bible is the Catholic Church. She is a mystery because she has hidden throughout history as an angel of light, coming under the pretense of good or as an angel of light as the previously mentioned Bible verses indicated. Consequently, in Voodoo, another name for its gods is mysteries.

Voodoo priests practice their witchcraft at night, usually from nine in the evening to about three in the morning—because this is the time when most people are sleeping. They can get into the minds of their victims at this time. The Voodoo priest I once knew told me that this was the purpose of working evening hours. They can work to cut off our dreams and sleep patterns and cause nightmares in children, among many other things.

I think it is best to give you a background about its origin and their rituals and practices so that we can better understand my point that we must leave the Catholic Church before it is too late. Those who remain in the Catholic Church will receive its plagues, as stated in the Bible, not to mention may go to hell for being associated with them. Here is the verse in Revelation 18:4 and Revelation 18:8 King James Version (KJV):

> *"And I heard another voice from heaven, saying, Come out of her, my people, that ye be not partakers of her sins, and that ye receive not of her plagues. For her sins have reached unto heaven, and God hath remembered her iniquities."*
>
> ~
>
> *"Therefore shall her plagues come in one day, death, and mourning, and famine; and she shall be utterly burned with fire: for strong is the Lord God who judgeth her."*

The Bible says God is against necromancy, and God is against people practicing ancestral worship. While Voodoo continues in Haiti under that name, many other religions branched off Voodoo and became known as; Santeria in Cuba, which means 'saint worship', Candomble and Macumba in Brazil, Argentina, Paraguay, and Uruguay and Taoism in Asia.

The mask of deception for all of these pagan religions is Mystery Babylon or the Catholic Church, but they are all one and the same. Voodoo and Santeria religions practice openly; while Catholics masks their identity by saying, they are Christian. How else could Satan deceive the masses, than to say we are all from God?

Remember that the Bible tells us the adversary comes as an angel of light. He masks his identity, and he does this by using the Catholic Church as his front. I reiterate that none of the saints worshiped in the Catholic Church are in the Bible. God tells us this in the following verse in 2 Corinthians 11:13-14 King James Version (KJV):

> *"For such are false apostles, deceitful workers, transforming themselves into the apostles of Christ. And no marvel; for Satan himself is transformed into an angel of light."*

The best way Satan can fool us into thinking something is from God is to mix Bible verses with his worship and claim it is from God. Those who do not know the Bible can be deceived by this. God frowns upon synchronicity and complicity with pagan gods and holidays. It is known as 'Spiritual Fornication and Idol Worshiping.' It is the reason the book of Revelation identifies Mystery Babylon as the 'great whore.' It is because she is fornicating with false gods.

When we mix any part of paganism with God's Word, I believe that we open the door for the enemy to come into our home and church. The following verse proves that there is a correct way of worshiping God as stated in verse John 4:24 King James Version (KJV):

> *"God is a Spirit: and they that worship him must worship him in spirit and truth."*

The 'truth' portion of this statement refers to the pure truth; nothing else should be mixed with it. Among the most glaring examples of this confusion, in my opinion, are Christmas, Easter, Halloween, Saint Valentine's Day, and Saint Patrick's Day. All of these are man-made inventions, created by the Catholic Church for the purpose of causing people—even Believers—to commit spiritual fornication without even realizing it. It is the apostate state that the church finds itself in in the end times—as predicted in the Bible in 2 Thessalonians 3-4. Does Jesus receive honor from pagan celebrations? He does not. There is a reason God placed the first commandment first on the list:

> *"Thou shalt not have no other gods before me."*
> *Exodus 20:3 King James Version (KJV)*

This idea was obviously important to him; He knew how the devil would deceive us so, for our benefit, he asks us not to mix false religion with true worship. The Holy Ghost will not reside where truth and lies are mixed. Thus, the decision of which church to attend is an incredibly important one.

God is not to be mocked (Galatians 6:7 KJV). In several places in the Bible, he states unequivocally that he is a jealous God (Exodus 34:14 KJV; Deuteronomy 6:14-15 KJV). He will not tolerate being worshiped in the same way that any other god would be worshiped (Deuteronomy 12:3-4 KJV).

God instructed the Israelites on the method they were supposed to worship him. He warned them not to add to the process nor take away from it (Deuteronomy 4:2 KJV; 12:32 KJV; Revelation 22:18-19 KJV).

Notice his terrible wrath when the children of Israel tried to worship him through the golden calf (Exodus 32:1-9 KJV). They proclaimed a 'feast to the Lord' (verse 5), but he would have none of it! God was so enraged at the idolatry of his people that he considered exterminating the entire nation and starting over with Moses's family. Aaron's sons Nadab and Abihu burnt unauthorized fire to God, and he consumed them with fire. In other words, God killed them to show them that he needs to be respected and honored correctly.

Does Jesus, the only begotten Son of God the Father, tolerate worship that is based on a lie? He has tolerated it for quite some time because he is a merciful God, but I believe his preference would be that we do not do it. His word says to worship in spirit

CHAPTER 6: GUILTY BY ASSOCIATION

and truth. Many do not fully understand or consider the dangers of the non-Biblical traditions and customs that have taken over the commemoration of his sacrifice and triumphant victory.

I believe this is the reason for the state of apostasy the church currently finds itself in. The devil has gotten in and sucked the power out of the churches by convincing the leaders its ok to mix truth with a lie. The Bible states:

> *"But **in vain** they do **worship** me, teaching for doctrines the commandments of men."*
> *Matthew 15:9 King James Version (KJV)*

> *"Let no man beguile you of your reward in a voluntary humility and worshiping of angels, intruding into those things which he hath not seen, vainly puffed up by his fleshly mind"*
> *Colossians 2:18 King James Version (KJV)*

The previous passages prove the validity of my argument that we are not to allow ourselves to be deceived, and worship angels of Satan disguised in man-made statues with Christian names.

In doing so, we are voluntarily worshiping the angels of the devil. The devil's fallen angels hide behind the idols in the Catholic Church, Buddhism, and Hinduism, to name just a few. The verse above also states that those who practice such things are losing their reward. How are they giving this up? They are giving it up through the voluntary worship of angels—because they believed Satan's lies.

The longer we remain in the her the longer we are guilty of necromancy and idol worshiping. If we do not break free, we will be found guilty by association on Judgment Day. I say this to help us become free, out of love for you and not to judge anyone.

The following passage details his promise of love or retribution:

> *"Thou shalt now bow down thyself to them, nor serve them: for I the Lord thy God am a jealous God, **visiting the iniquity of the fathers upon the children unto the** third and fourth generation of them that hate me; **and showing mercy unto thousands of them that love me, and keep my commandments.**"*
> *Exodus 20:5-6 King James Version (KJV)*

He plainly says that the children of those who hate him will be cursed. Not only our children but also our children's children will be cursed if we worship any gods apart from him. There is a kinder promise from God that, if we turn from serving these idols, our children and we will have peace. He says that if we turn from worshiping other gods; He will show love not only to us but also to a thousand generations to come.

God says plainly in his word that he will not accept mixed worship, even if it was originally intended to honor him. It is offering what is abominable to him. Therefore, it does not honor him, Jesus says plainly:

> *"God is a Spirit: and they that worship him must worship him in Spirit and truth."*
> *John 4:24 King James Version (KJV)*

What is the truth? God's word—the Holy Bible—says Jesus, is the Truth (John 17:17). The Bible says that God will not accept worship when people combine it with pagan customs or traditions. He is speaking to the Catholic Church and all of its subsidiaries in the following verse, where Jesus says:

> *"In vain they do worship me, teaching for doctrines the commandments of men."*
> *Matthew 15:9 King James Version (KJV)*

Christmas observance is a tradition of men, and the commandments of God, as quoted, forbid it. Further, Jesus says:

CHAPTER 6: GUILTY BY ASSOCIATION

"And he said unto them, Full well ye reject the commandment of God, that ye may keep your own tradition."
Mark 7:9 King James Version (KJV)

This verse tells us God hates the deeds of the Nicolaitanes. The root word of Nicolaitanes is Nicholas. Consequently, there were five Popes named Nicholas in early church years as stated in the New Catholic Encyclopedia, pg. 383.

"But this thou hast, that thou hatest the deeds of the Nicolaitanes, which I also hate."
Revelation 2:6 King James Version (KJV)
~
"So hast thou also them that hold the doctrine of the Nicolaitanes, which thing I hate."
Revelation 2:15 King James Version (KJV)

Many Believers fall into this category, unfortunately; Catholicism is not the only religious group that celebrates these pagan holidays. Millions of Christians partake in these rituals as well. God hated it when the Israelites performed these deeds, and He is not happy when we do so today either. Nobody will ever actually know Jesus' date of birth. Many Messianic Jewish believers have traced it to Nisan 1 A.D. from the Jewish calendar. That, in my opinion, makes more sense than December 25.

Easter and eggs have nothing to do with Jesus the Messiah; the Easter Bunny is an idol created by the Catholic Church to take all the attention away from Jesus. As I explained in chapter four, we are ignorantly dishonoring God when we celebrate Easter. Santeria (which, as I said, is a child religion of Voodoo) has different names for its gods, but essentially the two religions have the same saints.

The names of their saints were changed because they had to go underground and hide under a Christian pretense so they would not be killed. Therefore, they were given names of the saints in the Bible while the priests knew the real African names of their gods. In the video documentary that I made for this book, there is a Santeria Priest that explains this truth. Both Haiti and Cuba have been in captivity for centuries because of their belief in strange gods, just as the Israelites were held captive in the hands of Egyptian pharaohs for seeking after false gods. Haiti suffers great poverty, and Cuba is in bondage to communism.

It is no wonder that God's judgment has been seen in these cities in recent years through hurricanes and earthquakes. Is it a coincidence that the storm touched down in New Orleans, a mecca for Voodoo? Is it a coincidence that Haiti, another Voodoo hotspot, was devastated by an earthquake in 2010?

The death toll from West Africa's Ebola outbreak has passed 10,000.[4] Many people living in this area practice worship of their ancestors and false African deities. It is the birthplace of these ungodly religions.

This area is, in fact, the birthplace of the African religion of Voodoo and the Yoruba religion of Santeria. Is it a coincidence that Cuba suffers under the yoke of communism when its official religion is Santeria? We cannot continue to worship Catholic saints under the name of Jesus Christ; we must choose one or the other.

We can look to any country in the world today and consider their belief in God. I can almost guarantee that, if they believe in a god other than Jesus, they are in captivity of some sort.

---

[4] As reported by The World Health Organization.

Countries in Bondage due to Idol Worshiping

COUNTRY	OUTCOME OF IDOL WORSHIPING	RELIGIOUS BELIEFS
China	Communism, frequent earthquakes	Buddhism, Taoism
India	Child slave labor at age 5, major earthquakes year round, children sacrificed as infants to their gods	Hinduism, Islam, Buddhism, Jainism, Sikhism
Haiti	One of the poorest countries in the world, the children starve	Voodoo, Catholicism
Cuba	Communism, food is rationed, clothing is rationed, poor living conditions, children enslaved; even after The U.S. President's deal, Cuba remains Communist.	Santeria, Catholicism
Laos	Communism	Buddhism
N. Korea	Communism	Buddhism, Confucianism, Taoism
Vietnam	Communism	Buddhism, Confucianism, Taoism
W. Africa	10,000 plus deaths from Ebola, children starve	Yoruba, Voodoo, Catholicism
U.S.A.	Democracy; however, since Allah replaced Jehovah as our head, freedom is slowly diminishing. NSA spying on our calls, next guns will be taken, eventually enslavement.	Islam, Hinduism, Catholicism, Judaism, Christianity
Iraq	Multi-Pary System, Suffers poverty and war	Shi'a Islam, Sunni Islam
Iran	Theocracy with Islamic idealogies. Often at war, suffers poverty	Shi'a Islam, Sunni and Sufi Islam
Syria	Socialist and often at war, suffers poverty	Arab Sunni Islam

In Jeremiah it shows how the Israelites hurt God's feelings. He provided everything for them and delivered them out of their enemies in Egypt. They were ungrateful and continued to follow other gods. In this verse, he states that he will make a new covenant which is through Jesus in verse Jeremiah 31:32 King James Version (KJV).

> *"Not according to the covenant I made with their fathers in the day that I took them by the hand to bring them out of the land of Egypt; which my covenant they brake, although I was an husband unto them, saith the LORD."*

God was very hurt by the betrayal of his own people as you can see in the previous passage. God has feelings just like we do. Many Cubans want to see their country free, but they do not know they are hurting God's feelings in looking to other gods for help. He says come to him and ask him. They cannot see that the answer is right within the pages of the Bible. Its timeless principles remain the same; we just need to apply them to our present day and age.

The reason for Cuba's incarceration is the same as the cause of Israel's captivity in Egypt. The Israelites continued to follow other gods, even after the Lord had delivered them from the hands of the Egyptians. It is not a political issue; it is a spiritual one that causes their enslavement.

The Lord showed me that this is also true of Cuba, as well as of other countries whose people worship other gods. Cuba can be free when Cubans stop practicing Santeria. Haiti and its population will be free when they stop serving their Voodoo gods. Nigeria's people will see their country prosper when they stop serving other gods. China can become free from communist rule when they stop serving Buddha. India can be free when they stop serving the thousands of gods they worship through their Hindu practices. The following verse tells us so in Psalm 33:12 King James Version (KJV):

> *"Blessed is the nation whose God is the LORD; and the people whom he hath chosen for his own inheritance."*

All countries throughout the world whose people suffer poverty, natural disasters, or harsh political regimes worship strange gods, and this is the reason God places them under captivity.

I foresee the same fate coming to America with the influx of Muslims who have arrived. We Americans have, in recent years, removed God from schools, government, and our belief systems, and we are slowly going into captivity.

The United States government has set up the Babylonian tower in the sky (the new World Trade Center) to whomever they serve and have changed laws in favor of gay marriage. They celebrated the Muslim holiday of Ramadan in July 2015 and shone a green light on the tower in honor of the god of the Muslims. The United States of America is no longer a Christian nation. There is a danger in this because it means that, since they decided to honor a god that is not Jesus Christ, God's hand of protection will no longer be on our country.

The majority of the Supreme Court were Catholics at that time, and if they were representing God, their vote would have been against the LGBT movement that is taking over America, because God says it is an abomination. An abomination to God means that their actions disgusts him, the verse is Leviticus 20:13 King James Version (KJV):

"If a man also lie with mankind, as he lieth with a woman, both of them have committed an abomination: they shall surely be put to death; their blood shall be upon them."
Leviticus 20:13 King James Version (KJV)

We will see major disasters unlike anything before here in the U.S. because of the ruling in June 2015 that forced all states to allow gay marriage. If gay people wish to continue with their lifestyle, then that is their business. In my opinion, their sexual orientation should be something private, just like heterosexuals' private activities.

Remember when the current U.S. President (2016) met with the Pope and they spoke of religious freedom? Now all of a sudden, since that meeting, religious freedom is being taken away from Christians and they are using the LGBT movement to do so. I believe they are working in unison.

God does not change, so if He destroyed Sodom and Gomorrah for that reason, what fate do you think the United States will have. Since government removed the one true God from our country, we have more crime, the value of our real estate has depreciated, our credit rating has reduced, and there are still high unemployment rates.

Droughts are a sign of judgment from God, as we can see in the following verse from the Bible in Deuteronomy 11:17 King James Version (KJV):

> "And then the LORD's wrath be kindled against you, and he shut up the heaven, that there be no rain, and that the land yield not her fruit; and lest ye perish quickly from off the good land which the LORD giveth you."

At the time of this writing, the state of California is in level D4, extreme drought, and uncontrollable fires. Sixty six million trees were killed by the drought in the California Sierra's since 2010 according to the United States Forest Service. I believe this is a direct result of the same-sex marriage laws in all fifty states. The Bible teaches that, in the end times, food will be expensive. California is a major supplier of produce and other products for the United States. If they cannot produce due to lack of water, the entire nation will suffer. I firmly believe the lack of rain is because of the same-sex marriage ruling.

There is evidence everywhere that the United States is not the free country it once was, and natural disasters are on the rise.

CHAPTER 6: GUILTY BY ASSOCIATION

Slowly but surely, our freedoms are being taken away. For example, the NSA can spy on us without a warrant. Our children have a grim future; they will inherit trillions of dollars of debt if something does not change immediately. Multi-billion dollar companies that we trust have sold us out to the government. Hackers from other countries have hacked into our government agencies, and large corporations accessing millions of U.S. social security numbers and private information in the last five to eight years like never before.

The examples in the Bible of how we should live are placed there because God loves us, and He knows what is best for us. They are there for us to reference and to know how we are to live according to God's laws. We are not meant to live by rules invented by a man, like those of the Catholic Church or doctrines of men in the government who support abortion and same-sex marriage.

The adversary has used governments and nations to accomplish his wicked plan by moving men throughout the ages to enforce the principles of his lawless government through nations and leaders who sell their souls to him for power and money.

Countries That Worship Gods Other Than Jesus

There is also massive Catholicism throughout Africa as well as in Haiti. They are in deep synchronism with one another, and this is the reason for their enslavement. Unfortunately, judgment by God himself will come upon Catholics soon for those who remain in this church.

Cuba is also a communist country; its food and clothing are rationed, and the living conditions are poor. Buildings are unsafe. Some are so old and decrepit that they could fall on those living in them at any time. The prevalent religion in Cuba is a mixture of Santeria and Catholicism.

North Korea is another communist country, and the people worship their 'divine leader' as if he were God. Their religious beliefs are rooted in Buddhism, Confucianism, and Taoism. Their people are enslaved to a tyrant leader.

The leaders of the world think that, because they get away with what they do, there is no God, but their day of reckoning will come.

Special Message to the Clergy

If you are a priest, nun, bishop, or cardinal in the Catholic Church, I especially want to reach out to you through this text. Jesus loves you, and he does not want you under the deception of your superiors any longer. The Bible says that those who teach others to sin and those who teach incorrect doctrine will receive more severe judgment and will be looked upon as the least in heaven for doing so.

I have found several verses that pertain to teaching others doctrines of men, like those that the Catholic Church teaches. I am sure your superiors have not told you this; therefore, I feel it is my duty to give you this information. I pray that the Lord will show you—just as he showed Martin Luther and so many others of the Catholic clergy—how to repent and turn away before it is too late as I did. Here is the verse in James 3:1 King James Version (KJV):

"My brethren, be not many masters, knowing that we shall receive the greater condemnation."

~

"Whosoever, therefore, shall break one of these least commandments, and shall teach men so, he shall be called the least in the kingdom of heaven: but whosoever shall do and teach them, the same shall be called great in the kingdom of heaven." Matthew 5:19 King James Version (KJV)

Once we know the truth, we are to turn from our transgression at once and never return to it. The word 'repent' comes from the phrase 'to turn from.'

If you are a priest, a nun, or any other member of the clergy or lay leaders, only you can do something about where you will spend eternity, and right now is the moment to do it. Do not let the devil use fear to keep you trapped in religion. Jesus Christ will set you free if you ask him to. The Bible says that you do not know if your life will be required of you this night. We never know what is in store for us; this means that we must urgently run from our transgression and find the living God, Jesus. Jesus is coming back so soon; all the signs are before us.

Once we die, we will not be called up from the dead as the Catholic Church teaches. Those spirits the enemy calls up are his fallen angels who come in the guise of dead family members to trick us.

All of the people who are in Voodoo, Santeria, Islam, and Catholicism are being lied to by the devil. We will not be coming back as a god when we die, and there are certainly no virgins waiting for us. The Bible does not lie, and it says that when we die we go directly to Jesus to be judged immediately into heaven or hell. If we are not 'born again,' we will not enter heaven. We need to get out of that church immediately and run to Jesus to save us.

> *"Jesus answered and said unto him, Verily, verily, I say unto thee, Except a man be **born again**, he cannot see the kingdom of God."*
> *John 3:3 King James Version (KJV)*

Why are the Ten Commandments in Catholic doctrine, different than those in the Bible?

First, I would like to provide a list of the official Ten Commandments written in the Bible. The Ten Commandments, found in Exodus 20:1–17 and Deuteronomy 5:6–21, are as follows. Numeral two in bold is the one the Catholic Church has removed:

1. "I am the LORD thy God, which have brought thee out of the land of Egypt, out of the house of bondage. Thou shalt have no other gods before me." (Exodus 20:2–3 KJV; Deuteronomy 5:6–7 KJV).

2. **"Thou shalt not make unto thee any graven image, or any likeness of any thing that is in heaven above, or that is in the earth beneath, or that is in the water under the earth. Thou shalt not bow down thyself to them, nor serve them: for I the Lord thy God am a jealous God, visiting the iniquity of the fathers upon the children unto the third and fourth generation of them that hate me. And shewing mercy unto thousands of them that love me, and keep my commandments." (Exodus 20:4–6 KJV; Deuteronomy 5:8–10 KJV).**

3. "Thou shalt not take the name of the LORD thy God in vain, for the LORD will not hold him guiltless that taketh his name in vain." (Exodus 20:7 KJV; Deuteronomy 5:11 KJV).

4. "Remember the Sabbath day, to keep it holy. Six days shalt thou labor, and do all thy work: But the seventh day the Sabbath of the LORD thy God: In it thou shalt not do any work, thou, nor thy son, nor thy daughter, thy manservant, nor thy maidservant, nor they cattle, nor thy stranger that is within thy gates: For in six days the Lord made heaven and earth, the sea, and all that in them is, and rested the seventh day: wherefore the Lord blessed the sabbath day, and hallowed it." (Exodus 20:8–11 KJV; Deuteronomy 5:12–15 KJV)

5. "Honor thy father and thy mother, that thy days may be long upon the land which the LORD thy God giveth thee." (Exodus 20:12 KJV; Deuteronomy 5:16 KJV).

6. *"Thou shalt not kill." (Exodus 20:13 KJV; Deuteronomy 5:17 KJV).*
7. *"Thou shalt not commit adultery." (Exodus 20:14 KJV; Deuteronomy 5:18 KJV).*
8. *"Thou shalt not steal." (Exodus 20:15 KJV; Deuteronomy 5:19 KJV).*
9. *"Thou shalt not bear false witness against thy neighbor." (Exodus 20:16 KJV; Deuteronomy 5:20 KJV).*
10. *"Thou shalt not covet thy neighbor's house, thou shalt not covet thy neighbor's wife, nor his manservant, nor his maidservant, nor his ox, nor his ass, nor any thing that is thy neighbor's." (Exodus 20:17 KJV; Deuteronomy 5:21 KJV).*

In the Catholic Catechism and most official Catholic documents (see the official Vatican website, Catechism of the Catholic Church), the first and second commandments are combined to read:

"I am the Lord thy God. Thou shalt not have other gods beside me."

To get the number of commandments back to ten, the tenth commandment is then split into two:

"You shall not covet your neighbor's wife" and "You shall not covet your neighbor's goods."
(La Santa Sede, updated 2014)

The numerals "1 to 10" do not appear in any ancient Hebrew manuscripts that contain the Ten Commandments; in these texts, no one officially settles how the commandments are to be divided. Technically, the second commandment contains two edicts: "Thou shalt not make unto thee any graven image," and "Thou shalt not bow down thyself to them." Further, the tenth commandment contains seven (related) prohibitions.

It is suspect that the Catholic Church would summarize the second commandment as *"Thou shalt not have no other gods before me"* and leave out "Thou shalt not make unto thee any graven image," and "Thou shalt not bow down thyself to them, nor serve them." Remember that the Catholic Church is accused of idolatry for its use of images and iconography and bowing down to statues made by men.

Due to the importance of the first two commandments, and because the ancient Israelites greatly struggled with idolatry, maintaining the precise and explicit condemnation of graven images seems to be the biblically prudent choice. The Catholic Church leaves out part of the second commandment, apparently trying to hide the fact that its images and icons are violations of that command. The Catholic Bibles do list the Ten Commandments, but they do not teach them and are not listed as in the Bible on the Vatican website under Catechism of the Catholic Church.

Why would they omit and change the commandments? It is clearly evident that the leaders eliminated the second commandment, split the tenth commandment into two, and changed the order of the text. As Exodus 20:3-5 King James Version (KJV)notes:

"Thou shalt not make unto thee any graven image, or any likeness of any thing that is in heaven above, or that is in the earth beneath, or that is in the water under the earth. **Thou shalt not bow down thyself to them, nor serve them***: for I the LORD thy God am a jealous God, visiting the iniquity of the fathers upon the children unto the third and fourth generation of them that hate me."*

When the Vatican gives its list of commandments online and on flyers, it omits the above verse. Why did the Papacy do this? The commandments were written on government courthouses and public schools. When its church members began asking why the church bows to idols and statues, the church ordered them removed from buildings so that people would no longer continue to confront it about its sin of bowing down to idols.

The Pew Forum on Religion & Public Life, June 2007 in an article titled *Religious Displays and the Court* stated the following:

> "The Supreme Court first addressed the constitutionality of public religious displays in 1980 when it reviewed a Kentucky law requiring public schools to display the Ten Commandments in classrooms. The court determined that the Kentucky measure amounted to government sponsorship of religion and was therefore unconstitutional. According to the court, the law violated the First Amendment's Establishment Clause, which prohibits government from establishing a religion and from favoring one religion over another, or from favoring religion generally over nonreligious beliefs."

The Church tells its members that they will translate and interpret the Bible for them, because they know that the best Catholic is an uneducated one. It is very sad that the Catholics do not read their Bible, if they would they would see that nothing they are being taught is Biblical. The missal books they have in the pews of their churches when we sit down are proof and in most churches they are sold, you have to pay for them. I have not seen a Bible in any Catholic Church I have ever visited. Therefore, the best Catholic, in their eyes, does not read the Bible.

The reason people like William Tyndale and John Wycliffe died was because they translated the Bible from Greek and Hebrew into English. This was a big threat to the Catholic Church because they maintained that it should be in Latin and that only they could interpret it.

Unfortunately, in those days, the Church had supreme authority and Mr. Tyndale was strangled and burnt at the stake for translating the Bible into English. In those days it was the only Bible translated from the oritinal text, not the Catholic version of the Bible.

The second commandment was intentionally changed because it educates people about the truth. It commits a major indictment against the Catholic Church of the graven images that fill their sacred spaces. Everywhere we find graven images of Mary, Lazarus, Jesus, and many others.

The Catholic Church does not want us to know that, when we bow down to its idols, we are worshiping their gods. As I mentioned earlier, they are practitioners of necromancy and Santeria and Voodoo, they had to hide their craft in order to avoid being killed in early history. In order to mask their religion, they gave their gods Christian names like Mary, Lazarus and Jesus and held services on Sunday and invited the lay people in to watch. The same is still done today during Voodoo ceremonies that take place in Miami and New Orleans. Anyone can walk in and watch their voodoo service, it is open to the public.

In bowing to their gods when we bow down in a church service, we are not only bowing down to the fallen angels of Satan, we are breaking the second commandment. The leaders are aware of this, and therefore removed this commandment from its catechism. If any church omits any of God's commandments in its teaching, get out immediately. Its omission is a red flag, indicating that it is not worshiping the God of Abraham, Isaac, and Jacob; they are worshiping a different god. A religious institution ought not to be afraid of its people knowing the Bible or anything it says. When any church makes itself bigger than the Bible, its priests and people are not worshiping God in the way he wants to be praised. Real Christian leaders believe in the Bible and want their people to read it, and should never say otherwise.

When religious leaders attempt to trump the authority of the Bible, parishioners unknowingly make the church their god and the Bible takes second place. Many people also worship their pastor; this should be avoided at all costs. The only one we should worship is Jesus.

The Catholic Church decrees that there is more than one authority: the authority of the Bible and the authority of the Catholic Church. They have their beliefs and their doctrines, and the Bible takes second place. You can read the beliefs of the Catholic Church right on the Vatican website at any time, they do not hide them. Mixture of false and true worship was practiced in Israel from the time of Moses and Aaron. God separated those who caused his people to fall back and stumble and scattered them away from Israel. I believe they fled to what we know of today as Africa, the home of Voodoo and Santeria.

Biblical doctrine states that if any man desires the role of bishop, he must be blameless and be the husband of one wife. However, the Catholic Church disagrees and states that its priests and officials should not be married. Although the Bible states that they should be married once, and remain married, the church says its decree—the Church has spoken! An institution that steps over the word of God is not a holy place; it is a man-made lie.

The Bible instructs us to let God be truth, and all others are liars in Romans 3:4 King James Version (KJV):

> *"God forbid: yea, let God be true, but every man a liar."*

The word of God stands, and no man on earth has the right to change it—no matter what he or she tells us. The Pope recently forgave all women who have had abortions, as if he had the power to do so. Only God has the power to forgive sins, and much more, transgressions that God hates and calls an abomination in this verse:

> "These six things doth the LORD hate: yea, seven are an abomination unto him: A proud look, a lying tongue, and **hands that shed innocent blood,...**"
> Proverbs 6:16-19 King James Version (KJV)

Why do they say we can be forgiven? It is because they claim to be God and to have the ability to forgive transgressions and if they say it is ok for us to do, we will disobey God. Ultimately, they want us to be guilty before God. The issue with this teaching is that without a preacher telling us what is wrong or right, there is no hope for humanity. We all need a shepherd to tell us when we do wrong. If not, the world will wind up in the chaos it is in today.

The Catholic Church also presents other reasons that they believe graven images are acceptable to God:

- They believe that the Protestant Church's condemnation of graven images is simply an extra commandment. It is not an additional commandment; it is the second commandment plain and clear for all to read.
- They say that God told the Israelites to put the graven image on top of the Ark of the Covenant. The Ark of the Covenant was unapproachable; only one person could enter the Holy of Holies, and that was a priest chosen by God himself. That priest did not tell God's people to bow down and worship a graven image. Before Jesus, nobody could approach God, only those chosen by God himself.
- The church also tries to justify its evil nature by saying that God told Moses to make a bronze serpent that would heal anyone who gazed upon it. God did not mean people to bow down to the bronze serpent; He did not say to worship the serpent above himself.

They twist everything because they do not rightly divide the word of God. Why would the Catholic Church go to such lengths to hide the truth if it was the actual church of God, as she claims to be? The church claims infallibility in the Second Vatican Council through Lumen Gentium, but history proves otherwise. They are known for murder in the Spanish Inquisition of many of true followers of Jesus, while they claimed to be doing it in the name of God.

To claim infallibility, you would have to be God. After all, as the Bible says, everyone sins Romans 3:10 King James Version (KJV):

> *"As it is written, There is none righteous, no, not one."*

The moment a person walks toward the pew; they are forced to bow down. We sin against Jesus every time we do this, and we break the second commandment, which explicitly states not to bow down to any graven image. Whether we realize it or not, this is what we are doing when we bow down into a pew. It is so ritualistic at this point, that people do not even realize their transgression against God. Churches that are truly from God, do not have pews where a person is forced to bow down.

They pray to, worship and carry the statues of Mary, Lazarus, and Jesus. The Bible says not to commit this sin. Remember, the first four commandments pertain to our relationship with God and, if we want to begin hearing from God, we must stop doing this. If we bow down to it, we worship it. There is an example of this in the Bible, in the story of Shadrach, Meshach, and Abednego. Their story is recorded in the book of Daniel, chapters 1–3.

These three men are known for their exclusive devotion to God because they refused to bow down to the idol, as the king had commanded them. They were delivered by divine intervention from the Babylonian execution of being burned alive in a fiery furnace. These three young Jews from the kingdom of Judah were inducted into Babylon along with Daniel at the time when the Babylonians occupied Jerusalem, approximately 605 B.C. This all took place during the campaign of Nebuchadnezzar II, during the first deportation of the Israelites.

King Nebuchadnezzar II of Babylon had a nine-story-high statue, made of gold, erected in the Plain of Dura (the region around present-day Karbala, Iraq). The statue was an image of himself, or possibly of the Babylonian god of wisdom, Nabu. When the project was complete, Nebuchadnezzar prepared a dedication ceremony to this image and ordered all surrounding inhabitants to bow down and worship it. The consequence for not worshiping the idol upon hearing the cue of instruments was an execution in the furnace.

During the dedication ceremony for the golden image, certain officials noticed that Shadrach, Meshach, and Abednego were not bowing down to the idol. They immediately notified Nebuchadnezzar. The king was enraged and demanded that the three men come before him. Nebuchadnezzar knew of these men because, not too long before, Daniel had petitioned the king to assign Shadrach, Meshach, and Abednego to oversee the political affairs of the province of Babylon.

Daniel was also extraordinary to the king because he had the gift to interpret dreams, unlike any of the Chaldean 'wise men.' Therefore, it is no surprise that the king would offer one more chance for these three Jews, who held such honorable positions, to show their patriotism to Babylon. It is a very interesting report, I challenge you to read the entire book to better understand what he endured. Their response was as follows in Daniel 3:16-18 King James Version (KJV):

> "O Nebuchadnezzar, we are not careful to answer thee in this matter. If it be so, our God whom we serve is able to deliver us from the burning fiery furnace, and He will deliver us out of thine hand, O king. But if not, be it known unto thee, O king, that we will not serve thy gods, nor worship the golden image which thou hast set up."

Nebuchadnezzar demanded that the execution furnace be heated seven times hotter than usual. Valiant soldiers of the king's army were ordered to bind the three men (fully-clothed) and cast them into the blazing furnace. The fire was so hot that the soldiers perished while attempting to throw the three tightly bound Jews into the oven.

The three men then fell into the fire. When the king saw what appeared to be not three, but four men in the furnace, unbound and walking about, he called to them to come out. He had seen the divine appearance of the fourth man and had been astonished at the sight.

As the three convicted men came out unharmed, King Nebuchadnezzar acknowledged the power of their God. He made a decree whereby people of any nation who said anything against the God of the Jews were to be killed. Shadrach, Meshach, and Abednego were then given promotions to high positions within the government of the province of Babylon.

In Christian tradition, one interpretation is that the fourth man in the furnace was Christ. The pagan king reasoned that their surviving the fire was unquestionably divine. Why did three Jewish men not bow down to the idol? Because they knew that whatever we bow down to is what we worship, and they made a choice not to bow down to anyone. They knew how important it was not to bow down or pray to anything or anyone other than God. When someone prays to Peter or Mary, they are worshiping him or her, not God. Peter cannot hear us; neither can Mary. Neither can Buddha nor any of our dead family members who have passed on.

The only one who can hear us is God because he is omnipresent. Satan is not; therefore, he pulls his fallen angels out of hell through Voodoo and uses them as his informants. Satan can also send his demons to us to confuse us and make us think it is a dead family member or friend to persuade us to do his will on earth. These entities can also perform miracles to make us believe they are from God and will fool people as stated in Matthew 24:24 King James Version (KJV):

"For there shall arise false Christ's, and false prophets, and shall shew great signs and wonders; insomuch that, if it were possible, they shall deceive the very elect."

People who die cannot see us here on earth, nor can they look at us or guide us as the Catholic Church teaches. If Satan were to tell us this, we would run to Jesus as quickly as possible. Satan wants us in hell with him. Anyone or anything we turn to besides God is our idol. There is nothing inherently wrong with any of these people or things; just go to God first, asking him in prayer for all our needs. Worship no man, because man will only let us down. Every man-made god will bow down to Jesus, as stated in the Bible in Philippians 2:10-11 King James Version (KJV):

"That at the name of Jesus every knee should bow, of things in heaven, and things in earth, and things under the earth: And that every tongue should confess that Jesus is Lord, to the glory of God the Father"

In the following chapter, I will show scripture on how God tells us that we cannot be part of, or bid anyone God speed who does not hold the doctrine of his Holy Word in the Bible. If you do, God's word says you will be guilty by association.

Chapter 6:

Guilty by Association

"If there come any unto you, and bring not this doctrine, receive him not into your house, neither bid him God speed: For he that biddeth him God speed is partaker of his evil deeds."
2 John 1:10-11 King James Version (KJV)

DOCTRINE, AS YOU may know, means a belief or set of beliefs held and taught by a church, political party, or other group. The law means the system of rules that a particular country or community recognizes as regulating the actions of its members and may enforce by the imposition of penalties. In God's kingdom in heaven, he has the final say, no matter what doctrines men have invented or believed.

The previous verse is telling us that if anyone tries to bring some other belief system to us, do not wish him well or say it's okay. If we do, we will be guilty of their sins, or, in today's vernacular, 'guilty by association.'

The following verse Revelation 22:19 King James Version (KJV) says that if anyone changes the holy scriptures of God or is a part of those who do, he will be taken out of the book of life. This shows how serious God is about anyone, especially a mere human, changing HIS word. It is a serious crime in God's eyes.

"And if any man shall take away from the words of the book of this prophecy, God shall take away his part out of the book of life, and out of the holy city, and from the things which are written in this book."

The difference between God's laws and man's doctrine is the one who imposes them and upholds them. God sustains his word in the Bible, and those who break his laws are lawbreakers. It is for this reason that the word of God cannot be changed; we have no authority to do so. Men can create doctrines and enforce them, but God's laws and his word still stand. Proof of this can be seen by God's judgments on people and nations in history, as I covered in earlier chapters.

Few people have written about the synchronicity between Voodoo and its Catholic cover-up. One of the significant few is J. Michael Dash. In his book *Culture and Customs of Haiti*, Dash writes:

> "Whenever the question of religion in Haiti is raised, it is invariably answered by the popular saying that Haiti is 90% Catholic and 100% Voodoo […] the practice of Voodoo is not only pervasive but interchangeable with Catholicism […] The vast majority of both the rural and urban population are Voodoo worshippers. The situation is further complicated because, although the masses are practitioners of Voodoo, they are likewise Roman Catholics (51)."

Later, Dash notes that:

> "The Catholic Church was accused, by the militant nationalists at the time, of collaborating with the Americans and of waging a campaign against the culture of the masses, in particular, the Voodoo religion" (53).

It is clear that the Catholic Church will wage war against those who know its secret and tries to expose the truth. Stenio Vincent, a well-known intellectual, argued strongly for the Catholic Church's involvement in Haiti. He denounced Voodoo as an embarrassment to the civilized world and as the primary cause of Haiti's backwardness.

In 1940, the Catholic Church began a campaign against Voodoo, led by Elie Lescot, the former President of Haiti. Duvalier, better known as Papa Doc, was the President of Haiti from 1957 to 1971 and forcefully converted the Roman Catholic Church to Haitian standards, making them pliant to his will. In 1959, he expelled troublesome foreign priests. In November 1960, Duvalier expelled Port-au-Prince Archbishop François Poirier. Two months later, he expelled Rémy Augustin, Poirier's replacement, and the country's sole native bishop, showing that concern for his personal power trumped his idealist beliefs. The Pope responded by excommunicating him. Duvalier then expelled the Bishop of Gonaïves, who had been repressing expressions of Voodoo in his diocese. In 1964, Duvalier expelled the entire Jesuit order. Not that losing the Papal blessing seems to have caused Duvalier excessive worry.

In return for an end to repression of the Haitian Church (but not the Haitian people), the Pope lifted the excommunication and presented Duvalier with one of his greatest victories. The 1966 Concordat granted him the power to nominate an indigenous hierarchy, the first ever in Haiti. As a result, the archbishop, all six bishops and most other church leaders in Haiti became Haitian, with loyalty to the Duvalier regime. An expert on Haiti has claimed that Duvalier even had Macoutes, which were among the Catholic priests to infiltrate and inform him of what was going on.[5] A 'Tonton Macoute' was a member of the Haitian paramilitary force created in 1959 by dictator François 'Papa Doc' Duvalier. It is said that they killed between thirty and sixty thousand people in their time, and the entire nation was scared of them.

In conclusion, as we can see both organized religions operate similarly with a force and an exorbitant desire for control and power. Their doctrines are not the same as God's doctrine in the Bible. Therefore, no association between Christianity and Voodoo is necessary. Even many Haitian pastors I know of today believe that Voodoo is from God. We are not to allow those who believe these false doctrines into our churches until they fully understand that Voodoo is not from God as they have been mistaught.

Many people believe that the syncretism between Voodoo and Catholicism started in Haiti, but this is not the case. They were always the same. The only difference is that once they used to practice in Africa, and now they practice this religion in Haiti. Voodoo practices its rituals openly, and Catholics practice occultly. The Catholic Church tried to quieten the Haitians but did not succeed.

Then, of course, there is other more visible evidence that the Catholic Church is an occult practice—namely sun worship. In the images to follow, we will see a cross with the sun around it that is a staple and symbol of the Catholic Church. I do not think they could make their occult practices any more obvious than the fact that they walk around holding crosses with the sun around it. It is

---

[5] As a side note, Duvalier died on October 4, 2014, during the time I was writing this book. May God have mercy on his soul.

my suspicion that their followers have been bewitched through infant baptism, the partaking of communion wafers, and Ash Wednesday. Placing a cross on someone's forehead is a form of mark written about in the Bible in the following verse:

*"And he causeth all, both small and great, rich and poor, free and bond, to receive a mark in their right hand, **or** in their foreheads:"*
Revelation 13:16 King James Version (KJV)

Satan marks them with an X as his because he will claim them and collect them at a later point. This mark is to mark his territory; we must not allow them to do this to us. The Pope toured South America recently. On July 5, 2015, in his first speech in Ecuador, he stated:

"We associate Jesus with the sun and the moon and all the stars in our religion."

He admitted they relate Jesus to the sun and the moon to the Church. Islam also uses the moon as her symbol, proving that the serpent leaves a trail wherever he goes thankfully and this allows us to identify him.

The Bible teaches against this, as we can see in the following verse in Deuteronomy 4:19 King James Version (KJV):

"And lest thou lift up thine eyes unto heaven, and when thou seest the sun, and the moon, and the stars, even all the host of heaven, shouldest be driven to worship them, and serve them, which the Lord thy God hath divided unto all nations under the whole heaven."

~

*"And hath gone and served other gods, and worshiped them, either the sun, or moon, or any of the host of Heaven, which **I have not commanded**;"*
Deuteronomy 17:3 King James Version (KJV)

The cross with the sun in the center, is on most Catholic steeples and is indicative of sun worship. In Voodoo, Legba (means sun god in the Fon language) is the master of the crossroads and no ceremony can take place without inviting him first. Legba's symbol or "veve" in Voodoo, is the cross with what looks like a sun in the center and two fishes riding up its poles. It is the same sundial in the center of the cross that sits on the Catholic Churches. Remember, the serpent always leaves a trail.

Jesus clearly said not to have any idols at all, in my opinion not even the cross. The wafer eaten during Eucharist is in the form of a sun. Sun worship dates all the way back to the time of the Egyptians.

God's word is clearly against graven images of any kind, because God already knew how the devil and his church were going to present themselves to us. It is for this very reason that we must obey God's Word and not man's doctrine. This pertains to Christians as well, many place this cross in their churches.

In my research, I also found scripture to show us that God is against sun worship and the burning of incense unto Baal. There was a king in Judah by the name of Josiah who became king when he was only eight years old. He was instructed by God to burn and kill all priests that worship and burn incense to Baal, the sun and the moon and planets. We can see that God is not in agreement with burning incense as is customary to this day in the Catholic Church to the sun, the moon or any of the hosts of heaven in the following verse in 2 Kings 23:5 King James Version (KJV):

> *"And he put down the idolatrous priests, whom the kings of Judah had ordained to burn incense in the high places in the cities of Judah, and in the places round about Jerusalem; them also that burned incense unto Baal, to the sun, and to the moon, and to the planets, and to all the host of heaven."*

CHAPTER 6: GUILTY BY ASSOCIATION

Papal Hat includes sun logo and is shaped like a Shark Head

Jesuit Logo includes the sun

Saint Peter's Basilica is a sundial

Saint Peter's Basilica not only looks like a sundial, but also resembles the eight-lined 'veve' (mystical drawing made of cornmeal) used in Voodoo ceremonies and is a doorway to and from hell that is drawn on the floor prior to spirit possession.

In Saint Peter's Basilica, there is an obelisk pointing straight up, right in the middle. Similar obelisks are in Washington, D.C., and several other cities around the world. In Voodoo, this same pillar is called a 'Poteau Mitan,' which means 'middle pole.' It resembles a pillar pointing to the sky and is similar to an obelisk or the steeples in many churches. The demons enter and exit through this altar from the ground (Hades) and come up through the pillar into the physical realm. Thousands of congregations in America of all denominations have steeples on top of their churches without knowing that they may be innocently practicing a custom that originated from Voodoo.

CHAPTER 6: GUILTY BY ASSOCIATION

Sun Altar in Basilica of St. Peter, Rome, Italy

The sun rises in the east, and is the true origin of Easter. Since they worship the sun, their altars contain the image of the sun like the one in the image above. This altar can be found in St. Peter's Basilica in Rome, Italy. Easter is celebrated in the middle of Passover as misdirection from the greatest magician on earth. It is meant to sway us away from God's commanded feast (Passover). As I explained in chapter four, the enemy did this to bring the power of the resurrection down to the physical realm and remove the supernatural power that it could have in our lives.

Satan even has true Bible believers practicing Easter, Christmas, and many more pagan holidays. God gave us these instructions because he knows what is right for us, and his ways are higher than our ways. I believe the mixture of pagan and true worship is the main reasons the church is in the apostate state that it is in. Most Christian churches in America celebrate these holidays the wrong way.

The Bible is very clear on this subject:

> "Ye cannot drink the cup of the Lord, and the cup of devils: ye cannot be partakers of the Lord's table, and of the table of devils."
> 1 Corinthians 10:21 King James Version (KJV)

~

> "He that is not with me is against me: and he that gathereth not with me scattereth."
> Luke 11:23 King James Version (KJV)

~

> "Now the Spirit speaketh expressly, that in the latter times some shall depart from the faith, giving heed to seducing spirits, and doctrines of devils."
> 1 Timothy 4:1 King James Version (KJV)

In Ephesians 6:12 KJV, God makes it very clear that our enemies are those who practice witchcraft and the occult, including necromancy. Many organizations claiming to be the true church of God practice these pagan customs in plain sight when they canonize their clergy and have crypts beneath their churches all over the world and honor the dead instead of God. This doctrine is contradictory to the Word of God, and we are to have nothing to do with any other doctrines. The Bible tells us that when the Antichrist sets himself up in the temple of God, he will claim to be God, and then Jesus will return and expel him in 2 Thessalonians 2:3-8 King James Version (KJV):

> "Let no **man** deceive you by any means: for that day shall not come, except there come a falling away first, and that man of sin be revealed, the son of perdition; Who opposeth and exalteth himself above all that is called God, or that is worshipped; so that he as God sitteth in the temple of God, shewing himself that he is Go ... And then shall that Wicked be revealed, whom the Lord shall consume with the spirit of his mouth, and shall destroy with the brightness of his coming."
> 2 Thessalonians 2:3-8 King James Version (KJV)

The enemy and his church will rise again in power under the second beast that I believe is Islam, through terrorism and the groups ISIS and ISIL. It is the Spanish Inquisition all over again under a new title.

America is also suspect to also possibly be the beast spoken of in Revelation. America has been practicing pagan customs for a long time now; When God's laws were on our buildings, God was merciful, but since we have taken his laws down, judgment is being loosed little by little. America has statues and monuments placed in several areas that are symbols of pagan traditions and sun worship, which date back to the Assyrian kings.

There is:

- The Charging Bull in New York symbolizing Ba'al worship.
- The obelisk in Washington, D.C., which in my opinion represents the middle post in Voodoo called 'poteau mitan.'
- The Statue of Liberty is the same woman with the 12 stars that is in most Catholic churches.
- The Baphomet Statue was discovered in Detroit, Michigan (recently discovered).
- The World Trade Center was rebuilt, and the Muslim spire sits on top of it. It confirms their lack of worship to the One True God, Jehovah, and it defies him.

The hand of protection that God provided to the United States has been removed. We are under attack, and it does not look like it will be improving anytime soon. We need to know who our enemy is, and how to defeat him.

In Creole, the name of the sun god is Gran Soleil, the 'Great Sun'. Even the wafer Catholics eat at communion, the Eucharist, is in the shape of the sun. Whether we realize it or not, we worship the gods of the Voodoo religion in partaking of this. Christian names were given to their gods of brass, wood, stone and gold so that they could worship openly and not be murdered for doing so.

The Voodoo priests held services on Sunday's and invited the public into their "Christian" services. The reason the truth is surfacing now and not in prior times is because we are living in the end times, and Jesus Christ is returning very soon. He is trying to prepare his people and bring them into true worship.

I have also found an interesting article online that I placed down below, which corroborates the fact that Saint Nicholas is Gran Soleil, or the 'great sun' god in Voodoo. The owner of the site, who is also a Voodoo priest, also admits in an article that the twenty-one divisions of Dominican Republic Voodoo have their origins in Catholicism and that they work hand in hand. The article even goes on to say that these Voodoo practitioners were chosen and references a Bible verse, *"Many are called, but few are chosen"* (Matthew 22:14 KJV), because I am sure he was told that Voodoo is from God, just as I was told.

Further reading will reveal the three ranks of initiation into Voodoo. One of them is called a Kanzo, where you have to go through fire. Here is an excerpt from the online article I found:

"The word 'Kanzo' refers to a particular part of the ceremony where **the person undergoes a trial by fire.**"

What does God say about passing through the fire?

*"For when ye offer your gifts, when ye make your sons to pass **through the fire**, ye pollute yourselves with all your idols, even unto this day: and shall I be enquired of by you, O house of Israel? As I live, saith the Lord God, I will not be enquired of by you."*
Ezekiel 20:31 King James Version (KJV)

Loas, The Haitians' Gods Or Mysteries

The 'mysteries' or 'loas' in Voodoo are divided into three rites, and can be further subcategorized into what is known as the '21 Divisions.' The twenty-one groups of loas are placed into one of the three rites: The White, Black, and Indian divisions. Following is a chart of some of the loas and their Catholic counterparts. I am displaying these so that we can see that Catholic saints and Voodoo saints are one and the same. What the church did was change the name to Christian saint's names to mask their deception and so that they could continue to worship the gods of Satan, or his fallen angels through Voodoo and not be discovered.

Following is a partial list:

HAITIAN LOA	CATHOLIC 'SAINT'
Candelina	Our Lady of Candelaria
Candelo Cedife	Saint Charles
Cachita	Our Lady of Charity
Clementina	Virgen Milagrosa
Centinela	Saint Sebastian
Danballah (serpent)	Saint Patrick
Ezili Ailá (Alaíla)	Our Lady of High Grace
Ezili Danthó	Saint Barbara Africana
Ezili Kénwa	Saint Martha
Filomena Lubana	Saint Martha
Ghuede Gran Bwa	Saint Jude and Saint Rafael
Gran Solié (great sun)	Saint Nicholas
Gran Toro (Toroliza)	Christ of Good Hope
Gunguna	Saint Ellen
Jan Bakéo	Saint Peter
Jan Ferro	Saint Marcos Evangelist
Kriminelo (Jan Kriminel)	Saint Sebastian
Papa Legba	Saint Rafael
Marassa	Saints Cosmo and Damian
Metresili	Our Lady of Sorrows
Niño de Atocha	Child of Atocha
Ofelia Balendjo	Our Lady of Mercy
Ogun Balendjo	Saint James
Ogun Fegai	Saint Jorge
Ogun Batala	Saint Martin of Tours

Altars in Catholicism and Voodoo contain the same elements: candles, flowers, statues, and the image of their god: Ezili Danthó or Santa Barbara Africana.

In his, book *Voodoo in Haiti: Catholicism, Protestantism and a Model of Effective Ministry in the context of Voodoo in Haiti*, Dr. Andre Louis states the following:

> "The Catholic Church apparently seems to hold up its doctrinal teachings in the churches. However, the method of indoctrination through catechism reaches a very limited number so that most of the Catholics are nominal Believers. This attitude reflects the interaction of Catholicism-Voodooism and its consequences."

He goes on to say that:

> "In Haiti, Catholicism and Voodooism are linked in deep syncretism."

As we read Dr. Louis's book, we will learn how he also claims that Catholicism and Voodoo are the same.

Look at the next two images, which highlight the similarity of their garments and hats. The African priest is wearing the fish or shark hat from the Dahomey kingdom—similar to the hat the Popes wear today. The African priest is also dressed all in white, just like the Pope.

Another god in Voodoo is called 'Bon Dieu,' and the sun wafer they eat has the same name in Catholicism. Some Catholic priests may or may not be aware of this. It is my guess that most do not, and are not told the truth by their superiors.

Pope or 'Papa' dressed all in white.

Voodoo priest also called Papa in Creole and dressed in all white.

Previous Popes have worn similar hats that resemble the fish hat, but in Benin, Africa, the origin of the African religions, it is actually a shark head. In Spanish, "El Papa" means father, and everyone refers to the Pope by that name. In Voodoo, priests are also called 'Papa' or 'God Father.' What does the Bible say about calling anyone religious "Father"? God put this in the Bible for a reason.

Consequently, all the saints or demons in Voodoo called up are also called by the name "Papa" and then the name of the loa.

> *"And call no man your father upon the earth: for one is your Father, which is in heaven."*
> *Matthew 23:9 King James Version (KJV)*

What Did You Baptize Your Child Into?

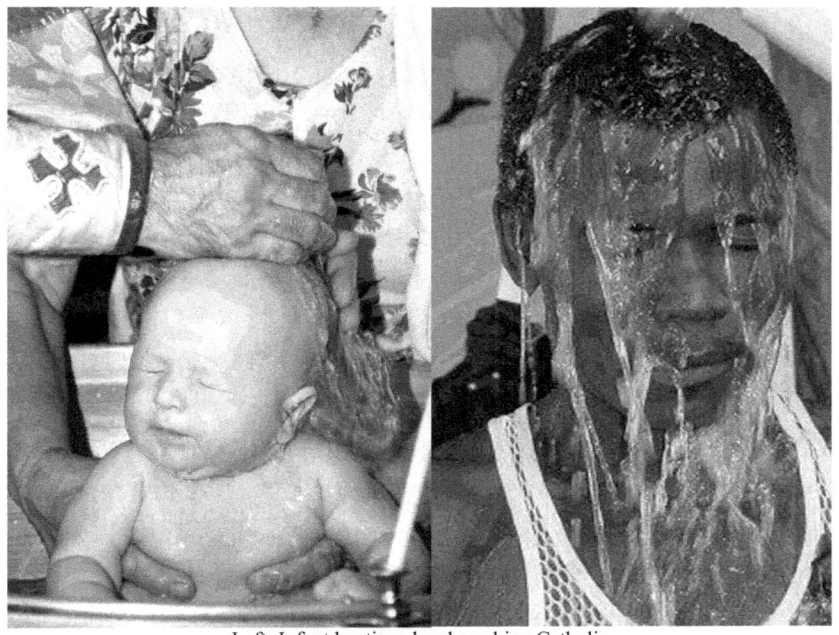

Left: Infant baptism, head-washing Catholic
Right -Lave Tate, head-washing Voodoo

Since baptism does not save us (only making a conscience decision to receive Jesus as God saves us), baby baptism is not necessary. The Bible tells us that babies go to heaven anyway if they die, so there is no need for infant baptism. We must then ponder why the enemy would want babies to be baptized. What is the motive behind such an act?

Having your infant baptized does nothing good for them. Since Catholicism is Voodoo in disguise, what you are doing is initiating your infant into the first phase as a Voodoo priest. The 'Lave Tet' is the first of three phases of initiation into Voodoo, and in English, it's called 'head washing.' I have placed references in the notes section so you can further investigate this subject, as I urge you to do so.

According to Voodoo, the head is considered the 'seat of all magic' for an individual. It serves as a vessel for their gods, as well as the other spirits that walk with a person throughout their life. In some Voodoo churches or houses, the Lave Tet is the initiation into the house and commits the person to that house. (If we conclude that Catholicism is Voodoo in disguise, then we can conclude that you have initiated your babies into the first phase of Voodoo.) Lave Tet is said among Voodoo practitioners to improve the ability to be possessed.

When a Catholic priest sprinkles a baby's head, they are initiating the child into Voodoo, whether they realize it or not. I am positive that they are doing so innocently and the majority have no clue that this is what they are doing. They are facilitating demonic possession, which is what the 'Lave Tet' does in Voodoo when the initiate is head washed. They have opened the door to the devil to come into their home, their life, and their child's life.

If and when Satan needs that child at some future point, the initiation has already been done during infant baptism. Allowing mind control and manipulation of the Voodoo priests over the initiates mind when they sleep. Voodoo priests work while you are sleeping. The Voodoo spirits follow the initiate their entire life unless we ask God's forgiveness and leave the church immediately. It is sneaky, shrewd, and horrific that the devil takes children at such a young age. He found a way to manipulate parents into willingly offering their precious babies up to Voodoo without ever being caught.

The Catholic Council of Florence stated that infant baptism was necessary for babies to go to heaven if they died, and if they were not baptized, they would go to hell. Many people started baptizing their children because of this false doctrine. Before this time, no babies were infant baptized. Jesus was baptized as an adult to show us how we are to be baptized; He was not an infant. The bewitchment by Satan takes place in the Catholic Church. They want to make sure you don't baptize your children when they are older—with the excuse that they have already been baptized as infants.

Only the devil himself could pull off a deception of this magnitude and never are caught. He has Catholics convinced that it will save their babies and through fear forces them to offer their children willingly as sacrifices to him while they are still young.

Not underestimating our enemy and the measures he will take to deceive us are the first steps we must take if you want to win the race that is set before us. Granted, Jesus did most of the work for us; but we still have to learn not to be deceived.

If parents want their babies to be blessed until they are old enough to accept Jesus on their own, both parents should hold the baby and give him/her to the Lord Jesus in prayer.

Here is an example of what Mary and Joseph did when they had Jesus:

> *"And when the days of her purification according to the law of Moses were accomplished, they brought him to Jerusalem, to present him to the Lord."*
> *Luke 2:22 King James Version (KJV)*

In the Law of Moses, women could not go into the temple until they finished their menstrual cycles. The verse above uses the term 'purification' to mean menstruation. Today many Christian churches do baby dedications and agree to raise their children to

know God in front of the entire congregation. Then, the Bible says that one of the greatest responsibilities we have as parents is to teach our children about God while they are still young.
Here are some Bible verses to back up my claim:

> "And, ye fathers, provoke not your children to wrath: but bring them up in the nurture and admonition of the Lord."
> Ephesians 6:4 King James Version (KJV)

> "Train up a child in the way he should go: and when he is old, he will not depart from it."
> Proverbs 22:6 King James Version (KJV)

What Do Christians Believe About Baptism?

Let me clarify that baptism does not save us; belief in Jesus and that he rose from the dead is what saves us. However, since the Bible commands us to be baptized, it is necessary that we be re-baptized in a doctrinally correct Christian church to be obedient to God's Word and to get to heaven. If you were baptized in the devil's church, you cannot get into heaven.

Any other baptism may have been an initiation in an occult religion. I also do not recommend taking communion with the churches of Satan, as this opens the door to him and allows him to bewitch you.

There are only two ordinances that the Bible makes clear are necessary—baptism and communion. Jesus himself was baptized as an example of how we should be baptized. He left us his command to remember his sacrifice by breaking bread and drinking wine until he returns. The bread and wine do not physically turn into his body and his blood.

If we have not participated in either of the ordinances mentioned above in a doctrinally correct church, it could be the primary cause we are not able to hear from God. If we do not have the Holy Ghost, we will not hear from God.

> *"Then Peter said unto them, Repent, and be baptized every one of you in the name of Jesus for the remission of sins, and ye shall receive the gift of the Holy Ghost."*
> *Acts 2:38-40 King James Version (KJV)*

~

> *"And Jesus, when he was baptized, went up straightway out of the water: and, lo, the heavens were opened unto him, and he saw the Spirit of God descending like a dove, and lighting upon him:"*
> *Matthew 3:16 King James Version (KJV)*

Jesus told us in the Bible that he would send the Holy Ghost to be his representative and is in the male format, 'He.'

> *"But the Comforter, which is the Holy Ghost, whom the Father will send in my name, **he** shall teach you all things, and bring all things to your remembrance, whatsoever I have said unto you."*
> *John 14:26 King James Version (KJV)*

~

> *"And I will pray the Father, and he shall give you another Comforter, that **he** may abide with you for ever, Even the Spirit of truth; whom the world cannot receive, because it seeth him not, neither knoweth him: but ye know him; for **he** dwelleth with you, and shall be in you. I will not leave you comfortless: I will come to you."*
> *John 14:16-18 King James Version (KJV)*

God told us he would send us The Holy Spirit to be his representative on earth, meaning those claiming to be God's representative on earth is blaspheming God's Spirit which is unpardonable.

> *"Wherefore I say unto you, All manner of sin and blasphemy shall be forgiven unto men: but the blasphemy against the Holy Ghost shall not be forgiven unto men."*
> *Matthew 12:31 King James Version (KJV)*

The counterfeit church refers to its 'holy' spirit as a 'she' because it is a different god that they worship, Mary. Their catechism refers to the church in the female gender at all times, which is why the Bible clearly identifies our enemy as *"a woman sit upon a scarlet colored beast..."* in Revelation 17:3.

Remember, in the foreword of this book I explained that Satan replicates all that God has and does this because it allows for the deception to be masked better. If God has angels, Satan has his angels. If God has a Holy Spirit, Satan has his spirit, but it is not holy. If God has saints, Satan has his saints, as the Voodoo priests call themselves. If God has a Bible, Satan also has his bible.

Those who do not have Jesus have no one to help them understand God's Word, and, therefore, they need idols, psychics, tarot readers, spirits of the dead, and fallen angels, mediums, and Popes to be their mediators. Christians do not consult mediums; we have direct contact with Almighty God, through Jesus Christ who lives inside of us.

"Now we have received, not the spirit of the world, but the spirit which is of God; that we might know the things that are freely given to us of God. Which things also we speak, not in the words which man's wisdom teacheth, but which the Holy Ghost teacheth; comparing spiritual things with spiritual."
1 Corinthians 2:12-13 King James Version (KJV)

The Vatican is home to the Catholic Church, and in the Bible God identifies the adversary's home by telling us it is a city infested with unclean spirits.

"And he cried mightily with a strong voice, saying, Babylon the great is fallen, is fallen, and is become the habitation of devils, and the hold of every foul spirit, and a cage of every unclean and hateful bird."
Revelation 18:2 King James Version (KJV)

In Rome, Italy, many demonic possessions take place because there are more than 800 cults in this one city alone. An account of an exorcism was detailed in a book written by Raul Salvucci: Cosa fare con questi diavoli? Indicazioni pastorali di un esorcista [Translation: *What to Do with All These Demons? A Pastoral Account of an Exorcism*]. He states there are 170,000 wizards residing in Rome, and that they have a following of some 12 million people who go to these wizards for guidance and bring in $600 million in annual fees charged to those seeking advice. It is all about money..[6]

All we need is Jesus; here is a prayer you can pray to the Father that Jesus gave us:

> *"After this manner, therefore, pray ye: Our Father, which art in heaven, Hallowed be Thy name. Thy kingdom come. Thy will be done in earth, as it is in heaven. Give us this day our daily bread. And forgive us our debts, as we forgive our debtors. And lead us not into temptation but deliver us from evil: For thine is the kingdom and the power, and the glory, forever. Amen."*
> *Matthew 6:9 King James Version (KJV)*

---

[6] Zenit Daily Dispatch, 1999 Increases in Cases of Demonic Possession

La Ermita de la Caridad, Miami, Florida
Photo Credit: Marisol Pareja 06/01/2014

The image above is of a shrine at a Catholic Shrine, *La Ermita de la Caridad*, in Miami, Florida. It is located right next to a middle and high school, where students have walked past it for years not seeing the witch pentacle on their grounds.

Just recently, the statue of Baphomet was discovered by accident on July 27, 2015, in Detroit, Michigan. This statue has the same pentacle on its chest as the one above. Its right hand is in the form of the Masonic hand sign that most occult practices use. Some even have a secret handshake. This Masonic hand sign is on many statues in Catholic churches and is not from the God of the Bible, Jehovah, or Jesus Christ—even though they have an image of their Jesus doing this hand signal.

Satan's logic behind this is if I put a picture of Jesus doing this masonic hand sign, people will think it is, in fact, the secret society of Jesus Christ. This is not the case; Jesus Christ had no secret societies, and his ministry was out in the open for all to see. Do you think Jesus knew that the enemy would claim Jesus had a secret society, and that is why Jesus taught out in the open? Jesus already knew what tactic the devil would use to deceive thousands of people.

The Jesus the Catholics worship is a different Jesus—one with long hair doing the Masonic "two fingers up" symbol. God warned us that other Jesus' would present themselves in the following verse:

> *"For there shall arise false christs, and false prophets, and shall shew great signs and wonders; insomuch that, if it were possible, they shall deceive the very elect."*
> *Matthew 24:24 King James Version (KJV)*

A church belonging to our Lord Jesus would not have a symbol that represents a demonic king from the Bible named Baal.

What Symbols Are Used in Christianity?
There are no symbols in Christianity. The Holy Ghost lives inside the believers once they are born again. We have no need for symbols or idols because we have the living Spirit of Jesus inside of us, and he guides us.

I know what it is like to be on the other side. I understand the desire to have a connection with God through an object. However, it is unnecessary. We are to have no graven images, in my opinion not even the cross.

Once we receive Jesus, he will set us free. He will speak to our heart. Having Jesus on our side is a far better choice than thinking that Satan has more power than God does because he does not! Serving Jesus is far better than serving the unclean spirits who will only lead us to the destruction of others and ourselves.

Additionally, we are guaranteed a place in hell if we continue serving other gods while Jesus promises heaven. The difference you will notice when you serve the one true God is that the God of Abraham, Isaac, and Jacob is the real and true, good God.

The Bible says that, if we ask anything in Jesus' name, it shall be done so long as it falls within the parameters of the will of God. Prayers are our way of communicating our desires. We need not buy candles, dolls, or other expensive items to get what we want from our God. We have no need to cast any spells or inflict our own will in a given situation. All we do is ask in prayer and God hears our prayers.

Another symbol used in occult practices is the pyramid, like the ones in Egypt. On the dollar bill, there is an image of this pyramid along with the pagan all-seeing eye of Horus, which is the same eye as the 'Holy See.' Popes are called Holy See—head of the all-seeing eye of Ra. The Pope is the Hierophant on the tarot deck. The All-Seeing Eye is supposed to be a universal symbol representing spiritual sight and the all-seeing eye of Horus and Ra, inner vision, higher knowledge, and insight into occult mysteries.

Following is an image of the Hierophant (a person, especially a priest in ancient Greece, who interprets sacred mysteries or esoteric principles) in the tarot deck, used in occult practices to foretell the future. The reason I am showing you this is to show you that their foundation is not based on Jesus Christ, but is based on a foundation of the occult which further proves my claim that Voodoo and Catholicism are one and the same.

In the image on the following page, there is a picture of the Hierophant Tarot Card who is wearing a triple tear crown and on the bottom of the card it even says "Le Pape" meaning The Pope. I also placed an image of Pope Bom with his triple-tier crown that is exactly like the tarot card. One thing is for certain; the Catholic Church and the heads of this church do not hide their beliefs. Their symbols and doctrine are available for anyone to read at the Vatican website and are in plain sight.

CHAPTER 6: GUILTY BY ASSOCIATION

Above, Hierophant Tarot deck.   Below, Pope Bom with triple-tier tiara

Can you see the hats are identical, and the card even reads Le Pape?

Left La Papesse Tarot Card   - Far Right Catholic Nun

As you can see their robes are identical, it is important to note that the women of the Muslim faith also wear a similar robe to these, only it covers their entire face. All three basically wear the same robes. Remember I told you before that the serpent always leaves a trail.

What Do Followers of Jesus Believe About the All-Seeing Eye?

We do not believe in it! Jesus sees and knows all that we do, he even knows how many hairs we have on our head:

> *"But the very hairs of your head are all numbered."*
> *Matthew 10:30 King James Version (KJV)*

He knows everything about us, even our thoughts:

> *"Neither is there any creature that is not manifest in his sight: but all things are naked and opened unto the eyes of him with whom we have to do."*
> *Hebrews 4:13 King James Version (KJV)*

God sees all the craft the witches do at night when they think nobody is watching. Even if you do not believe that, he is watching you:

CHAPTER 6: GUILTY BY ASSOCIATION

"Can any hide himself in secret places that I shall not see him? saith the Lord. Do not I fill heaven and earth? Saith the Lord."
Jeremiah 23:24 King James Version (KJV)

La Ermita de la Caridad in Miami, Florida.
Photo credit: Marisol Pareja 6/1/2014

La Ermita de la Caridad, a national shrine of the Catholic community in Miami, Florida, misinterprets the following verse and teaches worrship of Mary, instead of Jesus.

> *"When Jesus, therefore, saw his mother, and the disciple standing by whom he loved, he saith unto his mother, Woman, behold thy son! Then saith he to the disciple, Behold, thy mother! And from that hour that disciple took her unto his own home."*
> *John 19:26-28 King James Version (KJV)*

Jesus was asking John to take care of his mother since he was leaving her that hour. He did not say that worshippers should make a shrine to Mary, light candles to her, and bow down to her.

In order to understand the Bible, you need the Holy Spirit. Many people read it without asking Jesus into their life and receiving his gift and therefore do not understand it when they read it.

The enemy uses this verse to divert our attention away from Jesus. He focuses on Mary instead to keep our attention focused on everything else, but Jesus. It is one of many diversionary tools Satan uses.

Just like I was deceived for many years, millions are deceived today, and this is why I want to share my experience with you and tell you from the bottom of my heart that God really loves you, and he wants the best for you.

Jesus said that Satan is the 'Father of Lies.' Saints should not become the focus in place of Jesus—not even Mary. When people worship Mary, they deny Jesus as Lord. We are all aware of the verse where Jesus said that if you deny him, He would deny you before his Father.

> *"But whosoever shall deny me before men, him will I also deny before my Father, which is in heaven."*
> *Matthew 10:33 King James Version (KJV)*

CHAPTER 6: GUILTY BY ASSOCIATION

La Ermita de la Caridad Catholic Church, Miami, Florida
Photo credit: Marisol Pareja 6/1/2014

The sign translated, means 'To Jesus through Mary, Charity unites us.' Again, this church is insinuating salvation is through Mary and not Jesus. Jesus is always last, and Mary is in the front. This sign actually states Mary is the way to get to Jesus, making her the deity and denying Jesus Christ in doing so.

Belief in Jesus saves us, therefore, if the enemy can persuade us to believe anything else, then we are not saved. In claiming there is salvation through Mary instead of Jesus, will only lead us into hell. It is a trick most magicians use, called misdirection.

The famous "Ave Maria" song means hail Mary. Many people miss this fact, because it is such a popular song. It is obvious that they worship a female goddess instead of Jesus. The Christian names for their saints were given to their gods to cover up their true identity as voodoo priests to avoid being killed. During biblical times, witches were not accepted like they are today. Witches feared being killed by burning at the stake, therefore they did anything they could to hide their necromancy.

La Ermita de la Caridad.
Photo credit: Marisol Pareja 6/1/2014

Notice in the above photo that the cross is on the steeple with the sun around it. This symbol indicates sun-worship and in Voodoo that saint is called 'Gran Soleil,' or 'Saint Nicholas,' the great sun god that they call Legba in the Fon language.

CHAPTER 6: GUILTY BY ASSOCIATION

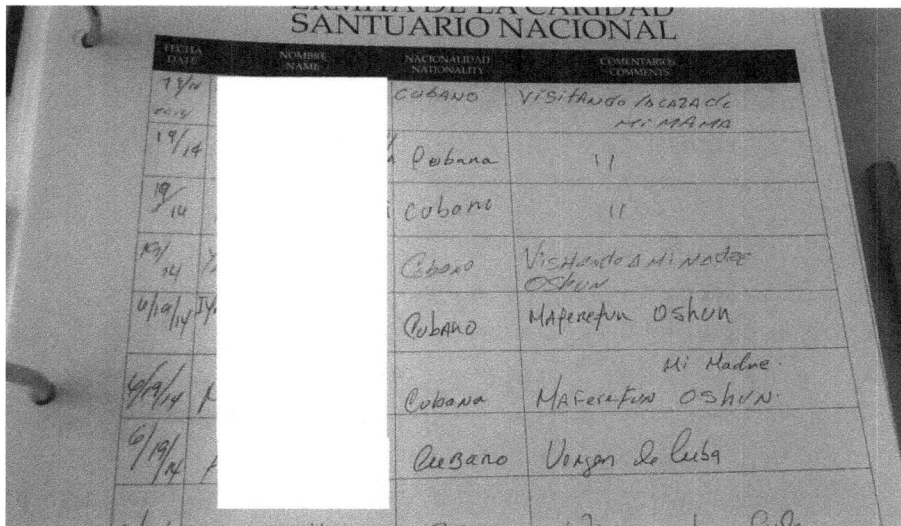

La Ermita de la Caridad sign-in-sheet.
Photo credit: Marisol Pareja 6/1/2014

La Ermita de la Caridad; 'M' represents Maitresse Ezili in Voodoo.
Photo credit: Marisol Pareja 6/1/2014

The interior of *La Ermita de la Caridad's* worship room. Take note of the 'M' stands for 'Maitre Ezili,' from the Voodoo religion.

According to Milo Rigaud, author of *The Secrets of Voodoo:*

"The veves represent figures of the astral forces . . . In the course of Voodoo ceremonies; the reproduction of the astral forces represented by the veves obliges the loas . . . To descend to earth."

She adds:

"Every loa has his or her unique veve or symbol, although regional differences have led to different veves for the same loa in some cases. Sacrifices and offerings are usually placed upon them, with food and drink being most commonly used. In ritual and other formalities, veve is generally drawn on the floor by strewing a powder-like substance, usually cornmeal, wheat flour, bark, red brick powder, or gunpowder, though the material depends entirely upon the ritual."

Left, Voodoo Ezili Danto, or the Black Madonna.
Right, the stained glass image of the Catholic Church, La Ermita de la Caridad, Miami, Florida.
Photo credit: Marisol Pareja 6/1/2014

The Black Madonna (Santa Barbara or Saint Barbara) above is said to have been at war with her sister Ezili Freda (who is Madre Dolorosa in Spanish or Lady of Sorrows in English) and stabbed her seven times in the heart while Ezili Freda sliced her face. It is for this reason that the Lady of Sorrows holds a bleeding heart with a dagger in it, and the Black Madonna above has a scar on the left side of her face. This woman has had many names throughout history, and comes in many forms, depending on which region and era she is worshiped in. Satan has changed her name throughout the centuries, but it is the same woman.

Satan pulled this fallen angel out of hell. These angels now demons, are the reason Voodoo is known to be so powerful. From experience I know that the only thing that will free you from these fallen angels is Jesus Christ. In other words, receive Jesus by faith and get baptized immediately. Do not wait to get baptized, these spirits do retaliate and will continue after you if you were ever involved with them. The Lord led me into a forty day fast immediately after I was born again.

La Ermita de la Caridad Python on stained glass in Catholic Church;
In Voodoo, his name is Danballah.
Photo credit: Marisol Pareja 6/1/2014

The Bible identifies Satan as the serpent. It was the serpent in the Garden of Eden that manipulated Eve and caused her and Adam to fall. In an earlier chapter, I mentioned that the serpent bites the horse's heel and causes them to fall back. Satan causes us to fall back while Jesus causes us to move forward to reunite us with the Father.

> *"And the serpent said unto the woman, Ye shall not surely die:"*
> *Genesis 3:4 King James Version (KJV)*

All pagans in every era have used the snake to worship as a symbol. The Egyptians used a sun supported by two asps as the emblem of Hor-hat, the genius god. The serpent with the wings and a globe stands firm over the doors and temples as a guardian god in Catholic churches worldwide. The entrances of Egyptian temples are decorated with the circle and the serpent.

Left, Erzulie Freda, the false African deity of the Voodoo religion; Right, Madre Dolorosa of the Catholic Church.

People in the Bible did not purposely allow demons to possess them. They did not consciously invite them inside their bodies to live within them like they do in Voodoo. Jesus had to rebuke demons out of many people during his ministry because they sinned and gave demons the legal authority to torment and harass them. He did not perform long ceremonies and purposely invite them into his body and become possessed by them as they do in Voodoo.

When the initiate of Voodoo is mounted (possessed) by Erzulie, she cries and weeps. The term 'Madre Dolorosa' in English means 'Lady of Sorrows.' Catholicism uses the same saint; it is just a cleaned up version to mask her identity. She is blamed for drug addictions, homosexuality, and, if angered, can drive her human victim through fruitless relationships. She forces the person to fall in love and become heartbroken over and over again and makes them often cry; thus her name Lady of Sorrows.

If you have had unsuccessful relationships, she may be the one causing this without your knowledge—especially if you were infant baptized by the Catholic Church or any of its offspring. If you are not born again of the Spirit of Jesus, she can possess you.

What Do Christians Believe About Mary?

Mary was a servant of God and served a unique purpose in bringing our Lord Jesus into the physical world. God chose her:

> *Matthew 22:14 King James Version (KJV)*
> "Many are called, but few are chosen."
>
> ~
>
> *Luke 1:38 King James Version (KJV)*
> "And Mary said, Behold the handmaid of the Lord; be it unto me according to Thy word. And the angel departed from her."

God states in the previous verse that Mary is a servant of the Lord Jesus. Never did she ask anyone to bow down to her and worship her above Jesus. Jesus suffered the bloodshed and the pain. He deserves all of our worship because he— not Mary—laid down his life so that we could live.

Where can we find accurate and reliable prophecy? Only in the Bible can the truth be known. Some books make the same claim as the Bible, but they have little to no true prophecy. The future must be known before it can be declared. These cults contain little or no prophecy because they do not know the future. A third of the Bible is prophecy. The Father has given us plenty of evidence to rest our faith upon.

Other Catholic and Voodoo Similarities

The Catholics call their services 'mass' which is 'misa' in Spanish. In Voodoo and Santeria, it is also called 'misa.'

Another similarity is the jars that hold people's souls that they use in Voodoo known as 'govi jars.' Catholics call them 'ampullas,' which means 'flask' in Latin. Huffington Post credited the Pope with a miracle because the dried blood of deceased St. Gennaro inside the ampulla, turned into liquid before his eyes. Why would anyone keep someone's dried blood in a jar and then kiss it? None of these satanic rituals is in God's Bible. The govi jars are the place they keep the souls of their initiates in Voodoo according to Bob Corbett who wrote "Introduction to Voodoo in Haiti", March 1988.

The priests in both religions also wear the same color clothing as Cardinals and Bishops namely scarlet, purple. The high priests wear white for the rada rite and black for the petro rite, just like the Pope that wears white and the Pope that wears black. Godfathers are given to the new baby initiates in Catholicism just as in Voodoo when a person is head washed, they have a Godfather assigned to them. They also both call on the same god, the sun god for Catholics or Legba for Voodoo. In the Pope's visit to Ecuador his speech clearly stated that they associated Jesus with the Sun and the Catholic Church with the moon.

An article in The New York Times from Wednesday, July 29, 2015 reported that a small silver box containing bones and pieces of a lead ampulla with a letter 'M' engraved on it had been unearthed. They discovered that this box was from the Catholic Church. The letter stands for 'Maitresse Erzulie,' whose signature letter or symbol is always 'M' in Voodoo and Catholicism. They engrave the 'M' on many items in both religions. It is on the glass image of the church window I showed you earlier.

The Crypts Beneath Catholic Churches

> *Numbers 19:13 King James Version (KJV)*
> *"Whosoever toucheth the dead body of any man that is dead, and purifieth not himself, defileth the tabernacle of the LORD; and that soul shall be cut off from Israel: because the water of separation was not sprinkled upon him, he shall be unclean; his uncleanness is yet upon him."*

Since both religions use oral communication throughout the centuries, I found it difficult to find evidence proving my claim that Catholocism and Voodoo are one and the same. Then, while watching television one evening, the Lord showed me a documentary about skeleton crypts found underneath Catholic Churches in Italy. Entire underground shrines were discovered. I was surprised to find such hard evidence against them. They have cemeteries beneath their churches and still bury the dead there.

Why would God's church have the dead beneath their church services when God explicitly says that you are unclean spiritually when you surround yourself amongst the dead in Numbers 19:13 KJV? I believe it is because the use of human organs and body parts is an essential element of the practice of Voodoo. Without human (or animal) body parts, their magic would not be as effective.

The human organs, along with Voodoo dolls and pins, are what the Voodoo priests use to inflict the desired pain on their victims. Not to mention they receive anywhere from fifteen to thirty thousand dollars for such rituals. Having the community bury their dead beneath Catholic Churches gives them very easy access to otherwise very expensive body parts, not to mention preventing them from getting caught digging up graves like they do today. I discovered that the Catholic Church owns several thousand Catholic cemeteries all over the world, independent of their churches. One human cadaver is worth about nine hundred thousand dollars on the black market alone.

Discovery News published an article that proves that Voodoo priests have been caught stealing from graves in Africa, the country of origin of Voodoo:

> **Grave Robbers Seek Bones for Voodoo Rituals**
> Dec 3, 2012, 07:52 AM ET // by Benjamin Radford
> "Over 100 graves have been dug up in the West African country of Benin, looted by grave robbers seeking body parts for use in magic rituals."

The fallen angles are being pulled out of hell by Satan and doing his bidding. They also appear as dead family members to trick people into ancestral worship. In Isaiah 8:19 KJV God says to consult him, not the dead. If God were in agreement with what the Catholic Church does, why would he have this verse Isaiah 8:19 King James Version (KJV) in the Bible?

> *"And when they shall say unto you, Seek unto them that have familiar spirits, and unto wizards that peep, and that mutter: should not a people seek unto their God? for the living to the dead?"*

Having an underground cemetery at their disposal must have made acquiring body parts for their practice very easy in the old days. Some crypts contained underground cities, especially in Naples, Italy. The residents pondered why they would have this in churches. There are many news articles all over the country about people being arrested for digging up graves in search of bones. The article I cited is just one of many. Not only do Poland and the Czech Republic have skull chapels, but also in Rome there is the Capuchin Crypt that contains more than 4,000 skeletons and corpses—believed to be the friars buried by their order.

The Catholic order insists that the display is not meant to be macabre, but a silent reminder of the swift passage of life on earth. The Bible is clear that we are not to worship the dead, we are to worship Jesus, who is alive, and whom we can access just by calling on his name and asking him into our life.

In the following verse, the Bible says we are unclean when we are near dead bodies:

"And there were certain men, who were defiled by the dead body of a man, that they could not keep the Passover on that day: and they came before Moses and before Aaron on that day:"
Numbers 9:6 King James Version (KJV)

Of course, if you were a practitioner of necromancy, to collect bones and skulls would not be out of the ordinary. If we were a follower of Jesus, skulls and bones would not fascinate us. That is not something clergy members would look forward to, I would hope. The angels said to Mary when she went to the tomb of Jesus:

"Why seek ye the living among the dead?"
Luke 24:5 King James Version (KJV)

It means that we will not find Jesus in tombs or dead still hanging on a cross. He has risen! He is Alive! He can hear our prayers; He takes them to the Father and intercedes for us. He is our mediator between God and man. Once we are his child, that is.

What can dead spirits do for us that the living God cannot? God's promise to us, once we side with him, is to be joint-heirs with Jesus of all that God the Father has given him. He will share his kingdom with us. What an incredible promise!

> *"And if children, then heirs; heirs of God, and joint-heirs with Christ; if so be that we suffer with him, that we may be also glorified together."*
> *Romans 8:17 King James Version (KJV)*

A friend who used to inscribe names on tombs for a living told me that a group of nuns in New Jersey once called him. When he arrived, they took him down to a crypt beneath the church and told him he was to say nothing about what he saw or heard. They told him not to tell anyone and showed him a corpse that had been preserved by mummification, exactly as the corpses found in Egyptian cultures in the past. It is clear in the Bible that Israelites did not practice mummification—which was not necessary after death.

Notable Catholic Churches with underground cemeteries:

St. Patrick's Cathedral	Manhattan, NY
La Paz Catholic Church	Quito, Ecuador
St. Ethelredas Church	Holborn, London
Christ Church Cathedral	Dublin, OH
Church of Santa Maria	Wamba, Spain
San Bernardino alle Ossa	Milan, Italy
St. Francis	Evora, Portugal
The Catacombs of Paris	Paris, France
The Catacombs of San Gennaro	Naples, Italy
The Catacombs of San Gaudioso	Naples, Italy

In the next chapter, I will prove Mary had no special powers during her time on earth, nor does she have any in heaven. She was a pure and chosen vessel of God, and found favor in God's eyes, but she is not to be worshiped.

CHAPTER 6: GUILTY BY ASSOCIATION

Chapter 7:

Mary, Co-Redeemer?

"And Mary said, Behold the handmaid of the Lord; be it unto me according to your word. And the angel departed from her."
Luke 1:38 King James Version (KJV)

MARY WAS JESUS' servant, according to Mary herself in the previous verse in Luke 1:38 KJV. God chose her for bringing forth the Son of God in her womb and caring for Jesus until the time came for his death and resurrection.

At no point in Mary's time with Jesus did she cure anyone of diseases or perform any miracles. At no point did anyone bow down to worship her while she was here on earth. There is also no place in the Bible that says that once Jesus has risen, we should go and pray to and worship his mother. The Bible says that the

Holy Ghost, who is the third Person of the Trinity, will be our comforter and our teacher, not Mary. Mary was married to Joseph and was a mere human being who had other children. It was not a different Mary that had these children like the Catholics claim. It was the same Mary who bore Jesus. The following verses tell us so:

"Is not this the carpenter's son? Is not his mother called Mary? And his brethren, James, and Joses, and Simon, and Judas? And his sisters are they not all with us? Whence then hath this man all these things?"
Matthew 13:55-56 King James Version (KJV)

~

"While he yet talked to the people, behold, his mother and his brethren stood without, desiring to speak with him."
Matthew 12:46 King James Version (KJV)

~

"After this he went down to Capernaum, he, and his mother, and his brethren, and his disciples: and they continued there not many days."
John 2:12 King James Version (KJV)

Mary could not be the savior if she explicitly states that her savior is God in the following verse:

"And Mary said, My soul doth magnify the Lord, And my spirit hath rejoiced in God my Savior."
Luke 1:46-47 King James Version (KJV)

Mary sinned just like all human beings and offered a pair of turtledoves and pigeons to be sacrificed for her transgression, as displayed in the following verse:

"And to offer a sacrifice according to that which is said in the law of the Lord, A pair of turtledoves, or two young pigeons."
Luke 2:24 King James Version (KJV)

CHAPTER 7: MARY, CO-REDEEMER?

We must believe God and his word over men's teachings, or we will be guilty of the same sin Adam and Eve committed in the Garden of Eden when they believed Satan over God.

One day a woman in Biblical times tried to force Jesus to exalt Mary in the following verse in Luke 11:27 King James Version(KJV):

> "Blessed is the womb that bare thee, and the paps which thou hast sucked!"

It did not work! Jesus responded with the following verse:

> "But he said, Yea rather, blessed are they that hear the word of God and keep it."
> Luke 11:28 King James Version (KJV)

Amen, Jesus! In Scripture, Jesus never called Mary 'Mother.' He called her 'woman' because she was a vessel to bring forth the Son of God. Nothing more! Mary, as pure and beautiful as she was, grew old and died, just like every other person.

When God resurrected Jesus from the dead, Satan suffered a major setback. Four hundred years later Satan developed a plan to use one of his favorite fallen angels, 'The Queen of Heaven.' He used this goddess to deceive the people for centuries. By 431 A.D., he had pulled her out of hell and renamed her 'Mary.' Satan continues to pull his fallen angels out of hell through Voodoo and the veves of cornmeal on the floor. The veves are on the floor, meaning they are pulling an entity from hell in the earth, not from a heavenly realm. Satan made the world believe that his phony virgin ruled Heaven as a goddess. Many people who believe this lie will go to hell because they chose to believe the lies of the Catholic Church over the truth in God's Word.

Mary's service to the Lord Jesus was over when He died. She is now in heaven and cannot see those on earth, nor can she come down to earth to perform miracles. The only one who is omnipresent is God, which means that he can be in many places at one time.

When humans die, the Bible says they go directly to judgment and stand before Jesus Christ. They cannot see people on earth, nor can they communicate with those on earth ever again. Ideas to the contrary are a big misconception that people have because of the teachings of organizations that do not believe in biblical doctrines. Calling up of the dead for advice is called necromancy, and the Bible is against it as stated in the following verse:

> *"There shall not be found among you any one that maketh his son or his daughter to pass through the fire, or that useth divination, or an observer of times, or an enchanter, or a witch. Or a charmer, or a consulter with familiar spirits, or a wizard, or a necromancer. For all that do these things are an abomination unto the LORD: and because of these abominations the LORD thy God doth drive them out from before thee."*
> *Deuteronomy 18:10-12 King James Version (KJV)*

Jesus was God in the flesh. During his time on earth, He did many wonderful healing miracles and cured the sick, raised the dead, and opened blind eyes and deaf ears. He healed people of many diseases and even gave the beggar who could not walk since he was born the ability to walk for the first time.

There is not one instance of Mary doing a supernatural or miraculous healing in the Bible. Mary was also never spit on, mocked, or whipped. She did not hang on a cross and die for you or me. Jesus did!

The Catholic Church has placed so much emphasis on Mary instead of Jesus that they have caused thousands of people to sin by worshiping and bowing down to 'Mary's' statue. The best magician on earth, Satan, performs sleight of hand or misdirection. Please do not fall for hs schemes any longer, he is causing people to break the second commandment of God. It is kindling God's anger and bringing entire nations into captivity.

There have been instances in the media of miraculous appearances of Mary. These appearances are not the real Mary; they are the fallen angels of Satan disguised as Mary holding a baby to fool us.

Please do not be so easily persuaded and fall for this lie like Mr. Loyola, founder of the order of the Jesuits, whose story I will tell you in the next chapter. I have to admit it is quite shrewd, and only the master deceiver would come up with such an elaborate plan by sending a sweet, innocent Mary holding a cute baby and calling it baby Jesus. I was fooled as well, so I understand and relate to those in this predicament on a deeper level.

Next, I will describe two decrees and declarations given at The Second Vatican Council and what they mean if you remain a part of the Catholic Church or any of its offspring.

Chapter 8:

Second Vatican Council

"And the woman was arrayed in purple and scarlet colour, and decked with gold and precious stones and pearls, having a golden cup in her hand full of abominations and filthiness of her fornication."
Revelation 17:4 King James Version (KJV)

DURING THE TIME I was writing this book, the Lord gave me a dream in which I was inside a Catholic Church in a meeting where Cardinals were present wearing red (Cardinals wear scarlet, Bishops wear purple).

Many people I knew from high school were there. They were almost in a state of stupor, walking as if they were zombies as they headed through a door that led to someplace awful; I am assuming it was hell.

Sitting next to me in my dream was a priest, who was dressed all in black, and he was terrified at what I told him. I could see the fear in his eyes that the enemy had placed there all the years he was in this church.

I softly told him, "Don't worry; they cannot harm you once you have the one true God on your side." He took the crucifix that was around his neck, kissed it, and said, "I hope you are right!" I then said to him, "Don't worry, and have faith in God."

When I awoke, I spoke the words "II Vatican Council" at no will of my own. It was the Holy Ghost speaking through me again and wanting me to know what the Lord wanted me to write about in this book, as I have prayed and fasted so he would reveal more to me during the time I was writing.

After reading some decrees and declarations, I summed up those decrees that would most affect the layperson in his or her walk with the Lord Jesus Christ and clarify why what they are teaching is not Biblical. Therefore, I have detailed most of the topics discussed at this meeting as well as the location, dates, and times, for your review and investigation at Wikipedia.com for the Second Vatican Council.

Second Vatican Council was held at Saint Peter's Basilica from October 11, 1962, to December 8, 1965. Prior to this council was the First Vatican Council, convoked by Pope John XXIII, and presided by Pope Paul VI. There were upward of 2,625 attendees.

Topics discussed can be found herein:
- The Church in itself, its sole salvific role as the one, true and complete Christian faith, also in relation to ecumenism among other religions, in relation to the modern world, renewal of consecrated life, liturgical disciplines, etc.
- There were four constitutions created during this council: Constitution on the Sacred Liturgy; Dogmatic Constitution on the Church; Dogmatic Constitution on Divine Revelation; Pastoral Constitution on the Church in the modern world.

- There were three declarations: Declaration on Christian Education; On the Relation of the Church to Non-Christian Religions; Declaration on Religious Freedom.
- There were nine decrees: Media of Social Communication; Catholic Churches of the Eastern Rite; Ecumenism; Pastoral Office of Bishops in the Church; Adaptation and Renewal of Religious Life; Priestly training; Apostolate of the Laity; Mission Activity of the Church; Ministry and Life of Priests.

A synopsis of the decrees and declarations of significant value to Catholics are as follows:

The Declaration of Nostra aetate states the unity of the origin of all people and the fact that they all return to the same God. Hence, all have the same goal in common (which is not true). It mentions that the Catholic Church accepts some truths present in other religions, including Voodoo and Santeria, Hinduism, Buddhism, and Islam. This institution accepts any religion except the true followers of Jesus and God's chosen people, the Jews. Their ecumenical plan unfolding before our very eyes is proof of this in, which the Pope stands against Israel and true Christians who won't partner with his one world order agenda in the name of terrorism.

The main purpose of the ecumenical council was to introduce Voodoo and other religions to the world so that the Vatican can declare all religions are acceptable including Voodoo and to say that the church is universal and not local. What better way to get us to practice their religion, than to say let us all unite and be one?

The Nostra aetate goes on to say that, the Catholic Church holds Muslims in esteem and then describes all the similarities Islam has with Christianity, including the worship of one God, the creator of heaven and earth.

It also states that Muslims respect Abraham and Mary and that they have great respect for Jesus, whom they consider a Prophet and not God. We know this cannot be from God because Jesus said that anyone who denies him would not go to heaven:

> *"But whosoever shall deny me before men, him will I also deny before my Father which is in heaven."*
> *Matthew 10:33 King James Version (KJV)*

~

> *"Every tree that bringeth not forth good fruit is hewn down, and cast into the fire. Wherefore by their fruits ye shall know them. Not everyone that saith unto me, Lord, Lord, shall enter into the kingdom of heaven; but he that doeth the will of my Father which is in heaven."*
> *Matthew 7:19-21 King James Version (KJV)*

The verse above shows us how to identify those who are not obeying God's commands, and it is clear that by their fruits we will know who they are. If they do good, they are from God; if they do badly, they are not from God.

> *"A **good tree cannot** bring forth evil fruit; neither can **a corrupt tree** bring forth **good** fruit."*
> *Matthew 7:18 King James Version (KJV)*

It is clear, unfortunately, that throughout history and even today the fruit of the Catholic Church is not good. Pedophile priests, murders in the Vatican, gay Bishops, murder of millions of true followers of Jesus by former Popes, pro-abortion and pro-gay stances they take and penance to pay your way out of hell are all bad fruit.

We must ask Jesus into our lives, instead of continuing to live in sin. In the Bible, Jesus himself states the following verse:

CHAPTER 8: SECOND VATICAN COUNCIL

"Jesus saith unto him, I am the way, the truth, and the life: no man cometh unto the Father, but by me."
John 14:6 King James Version (KJV)
~
"Ye cannot drink the cup of the Lord, and the cup of devils: ye cannot be partakers of the Lord's table, and of the table of devils.
1 Corinthians 10:21 King James Version (KJV)

We can choose to listen to God from his Word, or we can choose to listen to the devil that lies to us. The choice is ours and, while deciding, remember that it is no different from when the Devil told Eve "You will not surely die" and God told her she would die. Let us not be like Eve; do what God tells us to do and stop listening to the adversary who wants our soul in hell with him.

This text in the Second Vatican Council proves the Catholic Church handles the formation of the one world religion and government. Why else would the Pope meet with heads of state from every nation?

The most notable outcome of the Second Vatican Council is the **Dogmatic Constitution on the Church—Lumen Gentium,** meaning 'Light of the Nations,' which failed and is now called the United Nations. The Vatican, Kosovo and Taiwan are the only countries in the world that are not a member of the United Nations. There is no need for the Vatican to be a member since it is my belief that they are the head of the United Nations.

At the Second Vatican Council, they explicitly state that you are not saved without being a member of the Catholic Church:

"Whosoever, therefore, knowing that the Catholic Church was made necessary by Christ, would refuse to enter or to remain in it, could not be saved."

The Bible, which is God's authority on earth, says differently in the following verses:

> *"For by grace are ye saved through **faith**; and that not of yourselves: it is the **gift of God**:"*
> *Ephesians 2:8 King James Version (KJV)*

> *"And brought them out, and said, Sirs, what must I do to be saved? And they said, Believe on the Lord Jesus Christ, and thou shalt be saved, and thy house."*
> *Acts 16:30-31 King James Version (KJV)*

Belief in Jesus Christ saves us, not being forced into membership by any church. God gives us salvation as a gift, but we have to choose to receive his gift. The devil wants to rob us of this gift, so he forces his religion down our throat. If belief in Jesus saves us, and if the devil can persuade us to believe something else then we are not saved.

He is cunning! We cannot believe that Mary, baptism, or the Catholic Church saves us; if we do, we are not saved. We must believe that Jesus saves us and NOTHING else. Jesus gives all people the choice of free will. If we do not want him to be our God, then it is our choice. It is one of the best ways we can tell the difference between the church of God and the church of the adversary. If you recall, I mentioned in earlier chapters that everything God does, the adversary copies—including having his own church.

God is a loving God who lets us decide on our own, while the adversary's church forces his will upon the people. Therefore, to decipher which church or churches belong to the enemy, just look for the one that imposes its will on people by force. Then stay out of any that are called Christian and that partner with the one-world agenda in the end times, namely those in the World Council of Churches, as they will all be guilty by association.

It is apparent throughout history that there has never been any church that forces their will upon others greater than the Roman Catholic Church.

CHAPTER 8: SECOND VATICAN COUNCIL

The Catholic Church is responsible for the deaths of millions of faithful followers of Jesus Christ and Jewish people throughout history. During the Spanish Inquisition and the Holocaust, they tortured innocent women and men just for reading the Bible or for being Jewish. In the Bible, God says that this woman, or church, is drunk with the blood of God's saints.

The operating manual of the "Holy Inquistion" was called *The Malleus Maleficarum*, instituted through a Papal Bull by Pope Innocent III on December 5, 1484. It was the standard by which the Inquisition was to be conducted. The Spanish Inquisition was named the Inquisition because the priests would inquire of the people, and those who did not stand with the Catholic Church were tortured by various torture tools that the priests used. They called anyone who did not hold their beliefs were heretics and witches.

Followers of Jesus were tortured in several different ways as well. To name a few: burning at the stake is one of Satan's favorite forms of torture because he knows what awaits him is the lake of fire, eye piercing is another, others were suspended with ropes so he or she can be rotated on an exceedingly sharp point sticking into his or her anus while the rich stood by and watched through a glass window.

Women were thrown off of very high places and were victims of sexual abuse by the priests because they were sexually depraved through celibacy for the past 350 years. Celibacy is a doctrine of demons, and is the main reason for pedofile priests in recent times.

Just recently, The Child Abuse Recovery group found evidence that more than 350,000 children ages 2 to 12 were placed in septic tanks by nuns after they died from improper nutrition and illnesses in Canada, Spain, and Ireland. This was resported on June 7, 2014 by the Child Abuse Recovery.

The Vatican is known for owning over 18,000 works of art, having the most valuable paintings in the world. The collection is said to be worth in the billions. One artist who painted the interior of the Vatican was Michelangelo, who left many of his paintings to the Catholic Church. Had they auctioned one of those off for the children who were starving in these abbeys, but they did not. I would not want to be associated with an institution that does this to innocent children. Not to mention the thousands of pedophile priests caught molesting little boys in more recent church history.

I knew when I was 29—before I researched this organization—it was not the faith of people I wanted to be associated with. It is for this reason that God is reaching out to you through me, in the hopes of holding your hand and leading you out of the counterfeit church and into the real church of God through my personal experience and with what the Lord has shown me.

Many innocent members of Christian and Catholic Churches have not researched the church they go to very well, just as I had not when I was Catholic. Most members attend because their parents have persisted with this organization for several generations, and it is a tradition. Some are aware of what goes on and are in agreement with their actions and, therefore, remain in this church.

The Word of God tells us about the Roman Catholic Church and what is going to happen to her. God describes her as the harlot and Mystery Babylon due to her spiritual unfaithfulness to God in Revelation 17:1-18 on the following page:

"And there came one of the seven angels which had the seven vials, and talked with me, saying unto me, Come hither; I will shew unto thee the judgment of the great whore that sitteth upon many waters:" (Revelation 17:5 shows that waters translates into people and nations of all different languages.)

CHAPTER 8: SECOND VATICAN COUNCIL

"With whom the kings of the earth have committed fornication, and the inhabitants of the earth have been made drunk with the wine of her fornication." (The whore of Babylon will have great worldwide influence. Examples are: Concordant of 1929 with Mussolini, the 1933 Concordant with Hitler, The Pope meets with world leaders almost monthly to this date, and he does it in front of the entire world.)

"So he carried me away in the spirit into the wilderness: and I saw a woman sit upon a scarlet coloured beast, full of names of blasphemy, having seven heads and ten horns." (Pope Leo XIII in his Encyclical Letter of June 20, 1884, states the following: "We hold upon this earth, the place of God Almighty." This proves they are blasphemous. Scarlet is a color widely used by Cardinals. Seven heads are the seven mountains on which it sits, Rome was called the "city on seven hills." And the ten horns are ten kingdoms she will rule, but these will turn against Rome in the end.)

"And the woman was arrayed in purple and scarlet colour, and decked with gold and precious stones and pearls, having a golden cup in her hand full of abominations and filthiness of her fornication."
(The Vatican museum is filled with priceless ancient paintings, tapestries, gold, and jewels once worn by despotic kings. Purple and scarlet are colors worn by clergy; Catholic and Voodoo priests both wear purple and scarlet as well.)

"And upon her forehead was a name written, Mystery, Babylon The Great, The Mother Of Harlots And Abominations Of The Earth." (Voodoo gods are also called "Les mysteries." This has been a mystery until this book.)

"And I saw the woman drunken with the blood of the saints, and with the blood of the martyrs of Jesus: and when I saw her, I wondered with great admiration." (Roman Catholicism is the most persecuting faith the world has ever seen... Now she

hides behind Islam. She commands the Catholic and Islamic religions on all its subjects or they die, as in what was formerly known as the Spanish Inquisition, where they slaughtered millions of true believers in Jesus.)

"And the angel said unto me, Wherefore, didst thou marvel? I will tell thee the mystery of the woman, and of the beast that carrieth her, which hath the seven heads and ten horns. The beast that thou sawest was, and is not; and shall ascend out of the bottomless pit, and go into perdition: and they that dwell on the earth shall wonder, whose names were not written in the book of life from the foundation of the world, when they behold the beast that was, and is not, and yet is. And here is the mind which hath wisdom. The seven heads are seven mountains, on which the woman sitteth." (The woman is a city. Rome was built on seven hills. The Catholic Encyclopedia states: "It is within the city of Rome, called the city of seven hills, that...")

There is no doubt that the above scriptures are speaking of the Catholic Church. There have been plenty of Councils in history, but the one that God wanted me to focus on most is the Second Vatican Council.

Second Vatican Council's Dogmatic Constitution on Divine Revelation states the following:

> "....For Sacred Scripture is the Word of God inasmuch as it is consigned to writing under the inspiration of the divine Spirit, while sacred tradition takes the word of God entrusted by Christ the Lord and the Holy Spirit to the Apostles, and hands it on to their successors in its full purity, so that led by the light of the Spirit of truth, they may in proclaiming it preserve this Word of God faithfully, explain it and make it more widely known.**Consequently, it is not from Sacred**

Scripture alone that the Church draws her certainty about everything which has been revealed. Therefore, both sacred tradition and Sacred Scripture are to be accepted and venerated with the same sense of loyalty and reverence."

The previous text from the Second Vatican Council explicitly states that it is not Scripture alone that they believe. They are openly saying that they add their traditions over what the Bible teaches, and if their holy spirit tells them something different for the era they are living in, then they follow that spirit's teaching instead of the Bible. The Bible states otherwise:

*"But he answered and said unto them, Why do ye also transgress the commandment of God by your **tradition**?"*
Matthew 15:3 King James Version (KJV)

~

*"Beware lest any man spoil you through philosophy and vain deceit, after the **tradition** of men, after the rudiments of the world, and not after Christ."*
Colossians 2:8 King James Version (KJV)

God does give us the Holy Spirit when we become born again, but the Holy Spirit will not tell us to do something contradictory to God's word. He will guide us according to the word of God. The trinity works together, and God's Kingdom is not divided; they all work in synergy. God removed those who did not wish to work with him long ago, and their spirits are here on earth now trying to get us to rebel against God and his army with them.

The adversary's church, however, is divided into many different bits and pieces, which makes it harder to identify them. They have different rites, different Bibles, and different beliefs. Many priests were not in agreement with what they saw while in service to the Catholic Church and left to open their own denominations while still holding Catholic doctrines in certain areas. I mention the following churches only to show which denominations broke off from the Catholic Church. Most people who attend the different denominations have genuinely wonderful people in their services, and there may be many who are truly saved. Some are an offspring of the Catholic Church and others have recently collaborated with them in the end times.

The commonly known that were broken off from "Mother Church" are as follows:

Lutheran, Anglican, Methodist, Eastern Orthodox, Oriental Orthodox, Reformed, Protestant, Episcopalian, Presbyterian, Church of Christ, Calvary Chapel, World Vision, Vineyard Churches, Assemblies of God, Disciples of Christ, Jehovah Witness, and Mormons to name a few.

These churches were once separated from the Catholic Church, but in recent end times 'Mama' is calling her flock back home because she is gathering her army for the ultimate battle. When Jesus returns he himself will battle the enemy and his church that he has gathered. Imagine the surprise these followers will encounter when they see they were deceived and they have to face Jesus Christ in battle. Jesus said in the following verses what happens to a kingdom that is divided:

"And if a kingdom be divided against itself, that kingdom cannot stand."
Mark 3:24 King James Version (KJV)

~

"And Jesus knew their thoughts, and said unto them, Every kingdom divided against itself is brought to desolation; and every city or house divided against itself shall not stand:"
Matthew 12:25 King James Version (KJV)

CHAPTER 8: SECOND VATICAN COUNCIL

The Second Vatican Council took place in 1964, yet so many people still follow this church because they do not know what the Word of God says, and they do not study it on their own. Today we can read the Bible in as little as three months with all the different Bible apps that are out on the market today. The Bible tells us to do so in the following verse:

> "Study to **shew thyself** approved unto God, a workman that needeth not to be ashamed, rightly dividing the word of truth."
> 2 Timothy 2:15 King James Version (KJV)

Gaudium Et Spes - The Pastoral Constitution On the Church in The Modern World

This document has had an enormous influence on the social teachings of the wider Christian churches and communities, especially churches that belong to the World Council of Churches who have agreed and adopted them. This document came from the Second Vatican Council.

I would not recommend attending any of the churches that are members of the World Council of Churches. Doing so means we agree with their one-world-order agenda and the Catholic doctrine that is clearly not from the Word of God.

In conclusion, they are pushing the one-world religion and government agenda and will make peace with all other religions, as they have clearly been doing, especially through the Second Vatican Council. To the person who has not studied the Bible, the one-world agenda would seem to be a noble cause. If we were all on the right side—God's side—then it would work. Agreeing with the counterfeit church and its false doctrine and agenda is not uniting with God and his plan; therefore, it is against God.

The Catholic Church's sole purpose in establishing a one-world or universal religion and government is fueled only by their desire for power and complete and total control of our money, our mind, and our will. Their ultimate agenda is to form a one-world government and religion. They want to take all of our money (and inherited money as well) and do away with the family structure (same-sex marriage possibly because they cannot reproduce), as we can see happening before our very eyes.

The Antichrist and his church want to unite all religions so that he can easily bend them to do his will—that is to kill true believers in Jesus Christ and Jewish believers who do not wish to join them. The proof is what we are witnessing through Islam and the terror groups ISIL/ISIS. They are the groups that could be leading the new inquisition on behalf of the adversary and their army.

I honestly believe that there are many innocent people in the Catholic Church, and the leaders at the top are not telling them the truth but are keeping them in the dark.

Did you know that there are two popes in the Catholic Church? There is the Pope who wears white (in Voodoo this would be called the Rada Rite), which is the present Pope. Then there is the Black Pope, (just as in Voodoo, and they are from the Petro Rite, which is a darker, stronger force than the white). Some claim that the Black Pope is the one calling all the shots and is the top leader of most governments and organizations all over the world.

The Black Madonna whom they worship is from the Petro Rite in Voodoo. She is the woman who appeared to Francis Loyola, founder of the order of the Jesuits. Mr. Loyola believed the apparition he saw was from God, who called him to take on this task. The Black Madonna is the Black Mary holding the child and has nothing to do with God the Father or Jesus Christ; her name in Voodoo is Erzulie Dantor. The apparition was not from God, but was Satan in disguise and came in the form of a woman holding a child to get Loyola to do what he wanted him to do. Satan can speak to people, influence people and come as an angel of light—as the Bible clearly states.

God is a sovereign God, and I do believe he can appear to anyone he wishes to, but he will not send a woman holding a child and appearing to be Jesus' mother. Dead people do not come back from the dead; it is not them speaking to us, and it is the devil and his fallen angels who are fooling people into believing that it is their dead family members.

God left us his word, and that is how God speaks to us today. When we want something from God, we just ask him for it.

"Ask, and it shall be given you; seek, and ye shall find; knock, and it shall be opened unto you:For every one that asketh receiveth; and he that seeketh findeth; and to him that knocketh it shall be opened."
Matthew 7:7-8 King James Version (KJV)

Having been in both Catholicism and Voodoo, I can tell you that there is no greater high priest than Jesus Christ. He intercedes for us when we ask in prayer, and he takes our prayers to the Father for us. He is our Intercessor, our mediator, and our judge. All we need to do is give him our prayer requests.

*"Who is gone into heaven, and is on the right hand of God; angels and authorities and **powers** being made subject unto him."*
1 Peter 3:22 King James Version (KJV)

More than 85 percent of my prayers have been answered since I became a Christian in 2009. None of my prayers worked while I was in Voodoo; it is all a mask. If you were baptized into Catholicism, you have given them permission and access to your mind, your body, your spirit, your will, and your soul. Once we have the Spirit of Jesus Christ living in our body, they cannot affect us unless we open the door to them again.

Next, I will show you where it states in the Bible that all people in the counterfeit churches should get out of these organizations as quickly as possible for their safety—spiritually and physically.

Chapter 9:

Come Out Of Her, My People

"And I heard another voice from heaven, saying, Come out of her, my people, that ye be not partakers of her sins, and that ye receive not of her plagues."
Revelation 18:4 King James Version (KJV)

God is speaking to those who are members of the Catholic church in the previous verse because he loves them so much. He identifies whom he is speaking about when he says "of her sins." God goes on to say what will happen to her in the next verse:

"Therefore shall her plagues come in one day, death, and mourning, and famine; and she shall be utterly burned with fire: for strong is the Lord God who judgeth her."
Revelation 18:8 King James Version (KJV)

This verse clearly states how sorcery is used to bewitch the nations:

"And the light of a candle shall shine no more at all in thee; and the voice of the bridegroom and of the bride shall be heard no more at all in thee: for thy merchants were the great men of the earth; for by thy sorceries were all nations deceived."
Revelation 18:23 King James Version (KJV)

Many are saying that this prophecy is speaking of the United States of America, but I believe it to be the Vatican, the Roman Empire who has used her sorcery of Voodoo to deceive entire nations. The following verse says that Babylon has, in fact, fallen:

"And there followed another angel, saying, Babylon is fallen, is fallen, that great city because she made all nations drink of the wine of the wrath of her fornication."
Revelation 14:8 King James Version (KJV)

The first statement in the previous passage shows that they will eventually fall. The priests also fulfill other Biblical prophecies about the mark of the beast. The mark of Ash Wednesday that most people in the Catholic Church take is also another form of a mark of the beast. They call it lent, as in he is lending you out to bring you back to him at some future point, and the mark he places on their forehead is a cross or an "X." This is a form of a mark of the beast in my opinion; it is not a blessing.

I believe this is one form that the enemy uses to blind his followers along with taking the Eucharist every single week. I think this is how he keeps the laity asleep and unable to see the truth. There is an unholy way to take the body and blood as mentioned in the Bible in the following verse:

"For he that eateth and drinketh unworthily, eateth and drinketh damnation to himself, not discerning the Lord's body."
1 Corinthians 11:29 King James Version (KJV)

CHAPTER 9: COME OUT OF HER, MY PEOPLE

If you care for your soul as God does, put what I am saying to the test, stop taking the Eucharist for a few months and stop going into these churches. Then, ask God to show you the truth and to fill you with the Holy Spirit and see if you realize anything different when you read the Bible. Then write to me and let me know how it goes.

The main reason the current Pope was selected and the other stepped down, is that they needed a new image. He claims to bring peace and the unity of all religions. His angle will be to be the peacemaker of all humanity as he has clearly done.

The face of the church has been tainted by more than 16,000 cases in the United States alone of priests molesting innocent little boys. They need to 'clean up' the messes they have left behind. I learned that there was a Vatican banker who was let go because he swindled millions of dollars. They needed a Pope who will allow priests to get married, and who speaks out to their old Protestant brothers and asks them to unite once again, just as the current Pope has done already! Time will tell if he will allow priests to marry, or if it was just talk. Do not be deceived into thinking that they are better in any way; it is all part of the deception.

When the Bible speaks of a 'woman' in the only prophetic book of the New Testament, Revelation, it is symbolic of the Catholic Church. Did you know that the Catholic Church names herself as the one and only "Holy Catholic **Apostolic** Church?" Apostasy by definition means "the abandonment or renunciation of a religious or political belief." In Greek the word "apostasis" means defection. In their title they actually claim their apostasy. They say these are her four major distinctive marks or characteristics. You would literally have to be blind not to see that this church, is not the church of God.

If you recall, earlier I pointed out that the Catholic Church refers to herself in the female gender. God used the term 'woman' in the Bible way before the Catholic Church existed because he knew that they would do this before any of these events took place. Why was this text written in symbols? The Roman Empire was killing anyone who tried to spread the gospel of Jesus, and so his followers had to write in symbolically so that they were not killed.

The Catholic Church also always refers to itself in the female gender format. God knew this and inspired men to write about 'Her' back in 30 A.D. This just serves as more proof that God wrote the Bible.

Consider how clever Satan's tactic was with Eve in the Garden of Eden. He subtly made a suggestion rather than an argument to discredit God's authority, casting doubt about God's credibility. Satan asked, "Has God indeed said, you shall not eat of every tree of the garden?"

Through the tone and inflection of his voice, Satan implied that there was doubt that God told them the truth. This is shown by the way that Eve replied: she corrected him. She knew from the inflection of his voice that he was really asking a question and casting doubt. When she replied, she over-corrected.

Like a good salesperson, the serpent got his victim to agree with him, getting the victim to say, "Yes, yes, yes," and then, "I'll buy it!" Eve was already influenced when she gave her reply because she over-corrected.

Satan successfully magnified God's strictness in her mind, reminding her that the way is narrow. She began to agree with him, thinking about God in terms the serpent wanted her to think. She started to agree, saying, "Yes, yes, yes" to the salesperson's ploys.

Satan immediately minimized the penalty, telling an outright lie, "You shall not die" (Genesis 3:4). Then, to clinch the sale, he offered her a reward: "You shall be like God" (Genesis 3:5). What a price she paid! Satan offered a reward that must have seemed so big to Adam and Eve that they could not afford to reject it. What he offered was enough to reorient their lives.

They did not catch the complete significance of what he offered, but understood enough to know that it was big. He offered the opportunity for the self to become the dominating focus of life: "You shall be God." He completely reoriented their lives by turning their attention away from obedience to God and toward obedience to the self. He gave them the right to choose and to set the standards of right and wrong. They bought it hook, line, and sinker.

From that point on, humanity has viewed God as a rival and competitor rather than as a friend—someone with whom to compete and to outwit rather than with whom to cooperate, for they were now gods too!

Satan's tactic is given to us in the Bible. God tells us how he will do his bidding in the following verse; he will blind your mind:

> *"In whom the god of this world (Satan) has blinded the minds of them which believe not, lest the light of the glorious gospel of Christ, who is the image of God, should shine unto them."*
> *2 Corinthians 4:4 King James Version (KJV)*

Satan has many ways of enticing us away from spiritual matters and blinding us, through the glitter and glamor of this world. It is a false counterfeit light; many times we follow our senses to that which is pleasing to the eyes, and many times those things lead us to temptations and trials and away from God. Satan keeps us busy chasing after things we think we need so that we will not have time to seek God or to go to church. He wants to keep us busy, so our eyes become blind to his evil plan.

Just as Satan is busy, God also works hard with his angels and servants. In this great controversy, Satan is trying to blind our minds while God is trying to open our minds to his truth. His truth is written in the Bible; why do you think the enemy has attempted to alter that Bible and keep this truth away from us for centuries?

In the end times, the book of Revelation discusses the Antichrist beast of Bible prophecy. I want you to know that, through this beast system, Satan will wreak havoc during the last days of earth. Fire will come down from heaven, and miracles will cause hundreds, thousands, or even millions of people to think that Satan is God. The beast system is the body of governments that he is allied with throughout the world. The woman rides the beast means that he implements his plans through the governmental systems or via politics.

There is also speculation that the Vatican will confirm alien life forms on earth, but these will be his fallen angels in disguise.

Could The U.S. President Be Working with The Pope?

Has the U.S. President been working with the Catholic Church since before he took office? According to Wikipedia two years after graduating college, the current U.S. President(2016), was hired in Chicago as Director of Developing Community Projects, a church-based community organization originally consisting of eight Catholic parishes in Roseland, West Pullman, and Riverdale on Chicago's South Side. He worked there as a community organizer from June 1985 to May 1988.

From 2005 through 2008, the President was a member of the United States Senate. In December 2006, President Bush signed into law the Democratic Republic of the Congo Relief, Security, and Democracy Promotion Act, marking the first federal legislation to be enacted with the President as its primary sponsor. The President then appointed two women to serve on the Supreme Court in the first two years of his presidency—and they were of the Catholic faith.

CHAPTER 9: COME OUT OF HER, MY PEOPLE

The President has ancestral roots in Kenya, as his father was born there, and he was a communist. His family is of the Luo area, where the known religions are Islam, Catholicism, and African traditional religions of ancestor worship such as Voodoo.

The President and Vice President a professed Roman Catholic, was the first Roman Catholic (and the first Delawarean) to become Vice President of the United States. He initially had no desire to run because he did not want to lose his vote in the Senate.

Did the President single out Vice President Biden because he was a Catholic? He had been head washed as a baby, meaning that it would be easy for the Vatican to impose its will on him. Maybe he was singled out early in the race because he was a Roman Catholic and was under the influence of the 'puppeteers' in the Vatican?

Since shortly following the Vice President's withdrawal from the presidential race, the President had been privately telling him he was interested in finding a significant place for him in the administration. Vice President Biden declined the President's first request to vet him for the vice presidential slot, fearing the vice presidency would result in a loss of status and voice in his Senate position, but subsequently changed his mind.

In June 22, 2008, during an interview on NBC's *'Meet the Press,'* Vice President Biden confirmed that, although he was not actively seeking a spot on the ticket, he would accept the vice presidential nomination if offered. I found another striking similarity while I was reading *Papal Sin*, by Garry Wills. On page 13, Wills writes about a signature of the Papal Commission on March 16, 1998, in a book called *The Holocaust Never to be Forgotten*, by author Avery Dulles. Right beneath the title it says, "We Remember."

On the same day I read this information, I was watching the news and saw that U.S. President had just signed a beam at the

New World Trade Center in the same way: "We remember." I instantly knew that God was telling me to write about this striking similarity.

Is this same *"We Remember"* signature, 16 years later, a mere coincidence? The President had met with the Pope only two months prior to this signing. The practitioners of Voodoo used the President and the Vice President, placing them in leadership roles to help accomplish their next great feat of religious persecution in America through the LGBT movement. In a meeting on March 27, 2014, The Pope and President met privately for an hour.

In an article on March 27, 2014 titled *"Obama, The Pope Meet for First Time,"* CNN reporter Abdull Halmah states that "the two emerged with different stories about what they discussed; the Pope stated that they spoke about religious freedom and The U.S. President stated that they neglected to talk about that issue."

Since that meeting, the gay movement has been used to attack religious freedoms in America. Even more concerning is that suddenly, only seven months after the President's meeting with the Pope, we are now at war with the terrorist groups ISIS and ISIL.

Christians in America may experience their very own holocaust and Spanish Inquisition through the beast of Islam. Is it a coincidence that this term "We Remember" was used to reference two mass killings? It would be clear that those who are opposed to and hate Christians are those who side with the adversary and his army, as stated in the Bible in the following verse:

"For we wrestle not against flesh and blood, but against principalities, against powers, against the rulers of the darkness of this world, against spiritual wickedness in high places."
Ephesians 6:12 King James Version (KJV)

Just recently the Pope visited Cuba, and only two months later, the U.S. President lifted the embargo prohibiting trade with Cuba. This embargo had been in place for over fifty years, and the Cubans in Miami were protesting for days in the streets of Miami in 2014.

It is apparent that they are working together—the woman (Catholic Church) and the beast(Islam) of Revelation—concerning the Cuba embargo and on the religious persecution that will come to America. Could the Pope have asked the Castro regime to work with the United States earlier to avoid so many years of suffering for the Cubans? Could it be that the Pope meets with these heads of state to provide them with their orders? Why not ask Castro to free Cuba and remove communism if he is so well tied to all of these world leaders? At the time of writing this book, the Pope did the Masonic hand sign during his speech during his visit to America.[7] I believe a significant change in America will occur shortly after that.

> *"Who opposeth and exalteth himself above all that is called God, or that is worshiped; so that he as God sitteth in the temple of God, shewing himself that he is God."*
> 2 Thessalonians 2:4 King James Version (KJV)

THE MAN OF SIN REVEALED

The previous verse tells us that the Antichrist will sit in the temple of God and claim to be God. It has also been said that the Anti-Christ will be from the tribe of Dan. He will have Jewish blood in him and gain great power on earth, with ability to influence like no other has been able to before. As we know today, the U.S. President has had enormous influence in the physical and I believe in the spiritual world as well. I believe that he is from the tribe of

---

[7] September 23, 2015

Dan, since his parents are from Kenya and many already suspect that he may be the Anti-Christ and that the false prophet is the Pope. As you can plainly see through media, they are working in unison.

Those who have already received Jesus as their Lord will be raptured up before the tribulation time comes and before the man of sin is revealed. We will be spared of the worst events that will be coming to this world when the Holy Ghost of God is taken from it, and all that is left are the devil and his followers:

> "Then we which are alive and remain shall be caught up together with them in the clouds, to meet the Lord in the air: and so shall we ever be with the Lord."
> 1 Thessalonians 4:17 King James Version (KJV)

Is The Queen of Heaven still being worshipped today?

The Bible also clearly states that we are NOT to worship the queen of heaven (I have placed the reference below). From August 13 through the 18th, 2014, the Vatican released a public letter that can be viewed on the Vatican website; it is an entire page giving honor to the queen of heaven. It is an article that reflects their sentiment for South Korea, which had just experienced a natural disaster. They call upon the queen of heaven for assistance, not Jesus. The Bible clearly states not to honor the queen of heaven:

> "And when we burned incense to the **queen of heaven** and poured out drink-offerings unto her, did we make her cakes to worship her, and pour out drink-offerings unto her, without our men?"....So that the LORD could no longer bear, because of the evil of your doings, and because of the abominations which ye have committed; therefore is your land a desolation, and an astonishment, and a curse, without an inhabitant, as at this day."
> Jeremiah 44:19-22 King James Version (KJV)

God is clearly against us making an offering of any kind to the queen of heaven. The images below depict how they still offer cake offerings to the queen of heaven in all three religions.

Catholic Church altar

Santeria altar

Voodoo Altar –Notice the sun disk just as in the Catholic Church

CHAPTER 9: COME OUT OF HER, MY PEOPLE

Non-Biblical doctrines of the Catholic Church:

Non-Biblical Teaching	Biblical Teaching
Pope is God on Earth	Exodus 20:3 KJV "Thou shalt have no other God's before me."
Good works are meritorious for salvation	Ephesians 2:8 "For by grace are ye saved through faith; and that not of yourselves: it is the gift of God."
Original sin washed away with baptism	Hebrews 9:22 "And almost all things are by the law purged with blood; and without shedding of blood is no remission."
Pope has power to absolve sin and grant indulgences	Mark 2:7 "Why doth this man thus speak blasphemies? who can forgive sins but God only?"
We must pray to saints to intercede for us to God	1 Timothy 2:5 "For there is one God, and one mediator between God and men, the man Christ Jesus;"
Mary is Co-Redeemer	Isaiah 44:6 "Thus saith the LORD the King of Israel, and his redeemer the LORD of hosts; I am the first, and I am the last; and beside me there is no God."

In the next chapter, I reveal what we must do next to know with certainty that we can go to heaven when we die, and how we can start to hear from God on our own.

Chapter 10:

The Key To Breaking Free

"If you fully obey the LORD your God and carefully follow all his commands I give you today, the LORD your God will set you high above all the nations on earth."
Deuteronomy 28:1 King James Version (KJV)

WHEN WE OBEY God's commands, we become free! When I began obeying God and gave up Voodoo and chose Jesus, he healed me and not only set me free, but has given my life new purpose and direction that I would never have accomplished on my own. The key to breaking free is making Jesus our Lord. God tells us this in the following verse:

"Blessed is the nation whose God is the LORD; and the people whom he hath chosen for his own inheritance."
Psalm 33:12 King James Version (KJV)

He has directed my paths because I chose to obey him. When we ask our children to do something that we know will keep them safe and out of harm's way, yet they don't listen, how does that make us feel? That would make us angry, wouldn't it?

I am convinced that if we give up the idols of wood and stone and repent from idol worshiping, God will free many nations. Not only will he free them, he will raise up the nation that repents from its sins higher than all the rest, just as his verse above says. God does not lie; When he says something, we can believe him. He is the good God, and he wants to have a relationship with us. God has no grandchildren, only children. Here is a verse that states what God does if we disobey him and seek other gods:

> *"And the soul that turneth after such as have familiar spirits, and after wizards, to go a whoring after them, I will even set my face against that soul, and will cut him off from among his people."*
> *Leviticus 20:6 King James Version (KJV)*

The verse describes what I believe has happened to the Cuban people in the last 50 years. The official religions in Cuba are Catholicism and Santeria; this fact is not hidden. The beautiful culture and music of the Cuban people are very dear and close to my heart because I was born and raised in Miami, Florida. I grew up eating Cuban food. My best friend from childhood is Cuban, and their family loved me as their own. I even grew up knowing about Santeria and seeing it practiced on several occasions at their home even though I thought it was a bit strange to have parties for statues.

I can tell you from first-hand experience that I was involved in both of those religions in the past in one way or another, and Jesus set me free. God's heart is to set people free through his Son Jesus, and I know now that we cannot mix that with other gods because God will not accept this type of worship. Why would He? His Son suffered and brutally died for us, not anyone else! God tells us in the Bible that there are no other Gods Beside him and that he despises idols:

CHAPTER 10: THE KEY TO BREAKING FREE

*"I am the L*ORD*, and there is none else, there is no God beside Me: I girded thee, though thou hast not known Me:"*
Isaiah 45:5 King James Version (KJV)

~

*"Thus saith the L*ORD *the King of Israel, and his redeemer the L*ORD *of hosts; I am the first, and I am the last; and beside me there is no God."*
Isaiah 44:6 King James Version (KJV)

~

*"Tell ye, and bring them near; yea, let them take counsel together: who hath declared this from ancient time? Who hath told it from that time? have not I the L*ORD*? And there is no God else beside me; a just God and a Saviour; there is none beside Me."*
Isaiah 45:21-22 King James Version (KJV)

~

"Thou art become guilty in thy blood that thou hast shed; and hast defiled thyself in thine idols which thou hast made; and thou hast caused thy days to draw near, and art come even unto thy years: therefore have I made thee a reproach unto the heathen, and a mocking to all countries."
Ezekiel 22:4 King James Version (KJV)

~

"For when ye offer your gifts, when ye make your sons to pass through the fire, ye pollute yourselves with all your idols, even unto this day: and shall I be enquired of by you, O house of Israel? As I live, saith the Lord God, I will not be enquired of by you."
Ezekiel 20:31 King James Version (KJV)

~

"I will do these things unto thee, because thou hast gone a whoring after the heathen, and because thou art polluted with their idols."
Ezekiel 23:30 King James Version (KJV)

~

"And they that escape of you shall remember me among the nations whither they shall be carried captives, because I am broken with their whorish heart, which hath departed from me,

and with their eyes, which go a whoring after their idols: and they shall lothe themselves for the evils which they have committed in all their abominations."
Ezekiel 6:9 King James Version (KJV)

I placed many verses above so it is apparent and very clear that God is against idol worshiping, in fact he despises it and we are not to teach others to break God's laws.

He wants the countries that practice idol worshiping to throw away the man-made gods and worship Jesus. It is the breaking of God's second commandment that is causing the curse of captivity in countries like Cuba, China, North Korea, Laos, India, and Vietnam; soon the United States as well since foreign gods are now worshiped instead of Jehovah in the White House.

God deals with this sin in various ways. Immeasurably high death tolls caused by natural disasters are one form of judgment. He did this to the Israelites when they made a golden calf. They started bowing down to it and worshiping it. When Nadab and Abihu lit the offering in the censers themselves, their fire was profane and thus God was not in it. They prepared an incense offering upon kindling of their own and not of the holy incense from the sacred bronze altar.

Thus, in Judaism it was termed strange fire. Aaron's sons spurned the command to wait for holy fire and offered incense with profane fire. Anyone who altered the sacrificial system assumed a prerogative belonging to God alone. God determines the judgments that are carried out against those who violate His commands.

We see this happening in India today. Children in India become slaves at only five years of age. Indians worship thousands of man-made idols. China and India have suffered great earthquakes in recent years, where God uses the earth to devour those who are breaking this commandment.

Please believe the Bible and not what they tell you because they are not our friend; God is. The adversary and his workers want us to break God's law because they know it will bring judgment upon us and keep us captive and under the devil's control. Once we stop believing their lies, the devil and his fallen angels have no power over us anymore. We can be set free; I am living proof.

The fact that God is still causing high death tolls in countries where idol worshiping is rampant proves to you that I am telling you the truth, and so is God. Believe him or believe me; I am risking my life to tell you the truth—just as Paul and the Apostles did.

I know that I am a bit of an optimist, but God says that the blood of all those whom I do not tell will be on my hands if I do not. To be quiet and have their blood on my hands when I face Jesus or to die at the hands of today's Roman Emperors. This is the choice I had to make. The following verse says so:

"When I say unto the wicked, Thou shalt surely die; and thou givest him not warning, nor speakest to warn the wicked from his wicked way, to save his life; the same wicked man shall die in his iniquity; but his blood will I require at thine hand."
Ezekiel 3:18 King James Version (KJV)

This verse is exactly what the adversary does not want us to know. He wants us to be in trouble with God, just as if he is. Another way God deals with idolatry by taking those guilty of this transgression into captivity for extended periods. I believe this is what has happened to Cuba. I also believe that God sees that there is hope for the Cuban people.

Another form of judgment due to idol worshiping is death through disease. The death toll for Ebola in West Africa has risen to approximately 9,000, and more than 20,700 have fallen ill with this disease. The World Health Organization claims that six out of every ten people who contract the virus will die. Many people did not receive care, so the numbers increased steadily.

The only way to stop it is to repent from idol worshiping. This location is the birthplace of Voodoo and Santeria and the African ancestral worship of the dead or necromancy. The dead do not come back to give us advice; God can guide us, not dead people. Idol worshiping causes God to separate people from their homelands. This ancient biblical commandment holds the key to setting Cuba free and other countries as well!

I also see this as an opportunity for the Cuban people to be the leaders they already are. For example: One of the top FBI agents in the United States was of Cuban origin, and the many famous singers and actors throughout history. There are also many Cubans leaders who are politicians. Other countries can also be set free from disobeying the ancient commandment of idol worshiping if the Cubans would take the lead in the spiritual realm as well.

God blessed his people the Israelites when they gave up idol worshiping, and I know how much he has blessed me since I did. I know he will do it again if we just turn to him instead. Every instance in the Bible when the Israelites gave up their other idols and strange gods and sought the one true God Jehovah, their lives changed for the better, and they were set free several times. The problem the Israelites faced was that eventually a new generation would be born, and they would forget Jehovah again.

Christians United for the Freedom of Nations began praying for Cuba two years ago when I began writing this book, and now there is an open market and a U.S. Embassy being established there again; however, the country remains communist because again they are placing their faith in men and not God.

Once we know how the adversary thinks and how he lies and persuades people, we begin to understand that it is Satan himself that has Cuba in the state it currently is in—and he has used modern-day Pharaohs to do so.

Santeria and Voodoo are harming and hindering our countries' progress instead of helping free them. This practice is sleight of hand from the devil. His tricks are intended to steer us away from following and serving Jesus and his Father because he knows that once we do, we will be free; he does not want freedom for anyone—much less entire countries.

The Voodoo priest I was going to be initiated under is Cuban, and it is my firm belief this man holds the spirit of Satan on earth and lives in Miami, Florida. He told me an entity took over his body in 1980, and he has had no control over his body ever since. This is another reason I believe that Cuba is in bondage to communism.

Satan uses whatever means he can to lure us away from Jesus so that we will serve him and his lower dark angels. Misdirection is his most oft-used tool. He is the master magician in that he lures us away from the truth—Jesus.

To get my point across, I first want to discuss the definition of magic. Merriam-Webster defines magic as follows:

> "The art of producing illusions is by sleight of hand. Sleight of hand means skill in deception; skill in feats requiring quick and intelligent movement of the hands, especially for entertainment or deception; trickery."

The whole basis of magic is showmanship and theatrics. A magician waves his hand and distracts us, making us think that the magic is taking place in one location, while the real trick is happening somewhere else. **Misdirection** is a fundamental concept of magic.

The efforts of Satan are intended to misdirect us so that you will worship his fallen angels (the 'saints' of Satan's religions) instead of Jesus. This misdirection has caused entire countries like Cuba, China, Haiti, and the Dominican Republic to fall under slavery and impoverishment. Satan has misdirected the entire world, not only the above-mentioned countries. Worse, they don't know that it is due to idol worshiping or the worship of other gods.

When Satan and his angels were cast out of heaven by God, they needed to find a way to be worshiped as God is. They have strived for God's power since they were cast here to earth. Their one goal is to trip you up so that you continue to fall; the less you know about them and their plan, the better.

It is plain to see that if the Santeria gods could help free Cuba and China and all the countries that worship any god other than Jesus, they would have done so already. I can tell you why they have not done so; it is because they do not have the power to do so. God is the only one who can free these countries. I speak from personal experience that this is what is stopping all of these countries from being free.

Tomas Estrada Palma, the first President of Cuba, was known to be a Quaker. Although the Cuban people did not like him because he made contracts with the United States, when he was President Cuba was, at the very least, still free. Catholicism was the dominant religion when Castro came to power, but he did not promote it and banned religion in later years. Many Catholic Churches closed, and religion was not allowed.

When communist Russia stopped sending supplies to Cuba, the country took a hard hit. The people needed to seek salvation in something, and the Catholic Churches began filling up. It is my belief that the Pope of that time influenced Russia to cut off Cuba's resources so that they would purposely seek the Vatican's assistance. It was a shrewd move; it worked because the churches reopened and were full once again.

The adversary Satan had his heart on Cuba way before this time, though. By 1840, the majority of Cubans were of African descent, and Santeria had entered the mainstream when the early slaves came from Africa and brought their religion with them. Remember that the origin of Catholicism is Voodoo.

One reason the Popes throughout history have tried to make sure that Catholicism remains prominent is because they claim to worship Jesus with their lips, but in their hearts they venerate the same saints who those in Santeria and Voodoo worship. Essentially, they are the same. The Catholic Church has purposely distanced itself from the Santeria and Voodoo religion so that their secret would not be discovered.

It was not until the rise of the Castro regime that the country became enslaved, and it has remained this way for 55 years. His brother had more promising expectations for Cuba, but the country is still impoverished. The Cuban residents have not seen the change they were expecting, and Cuba is still communist.

Santeria (saint worship) and Voodoo (spirit worship) are based entirely on ancestral worship, or the worship of dead spirits, as mediators between the living and the dead. Practitioners are told that if they pray and give reverence to dead family members, and give them offerings, they will be blessed with whatever they request. God's word calls this practice necromancy, and it is a tradition that dates all the way back to the seventh century before Jesus came to earth.

It existed in Ancient Greece and Rome. Ancestral worship has had its greatest influence on African and Asian cultures throughout the centuries. Today it is practiced in many parts of the world, in places like China, Cuba, Nigeria, West Africa, Haiti, and—

believe it or not—in recent years, the United States. It was practiced in Ancient Egypt as well.

One thing God tells us about those who die is that their spirits immediately enter judgment and come into the presence of Jesus to be judged. Jesus is our mediator, and he is the only mediator between God and man. We do not need 'dead' spirits to tell us our future because we can talk with God directly. He left us his word for guidance on every subject as you can see:

> *"Let us therefore come boldly unto the throne of grace, that we may obtain mercy, and find grace to help in time of need."*
> *Hebrews 4:16 King James Version (KJV)*

The devil lies to people who practice witchcraft and tells them that God is unreachable, so people need to speak to dead spirits. This is not true; the previous Bible verse—Hebrews 4:16—says that once we receive Jesus as our Lord, we can come boldly unto his throne of grace and ask for anything we need.

The devil wants to keep our focus on him and his fallen angels, so we never see the truth in Jesus. The truth is that we can ask for anything that we need directly from Jesus once he is our God. The following Bible verse attests to this fact:

> *"If ye shall ask any thing in My name, I will do it."*
> *John 14:14 King James Version (KJV)*

The devil has been quite successful at his magic arts. He has pulled the wool over the eyes of so many, and I guarantee you that he gloats over his triumph all day long. He loves that he can deceive people, and he has been deceiving those who practice magic arts since long before Jesus came to save us.

Jesus made it so easy for his followers that the offer seems too good to be true. When I attended a church in Las Vegas one Sunday afternoon, the pastor told me what Jesus did for me. All I had to do was say a prayer and receive what he did for me; I would know with absolute certainty that I would go to heaven when I died.

I remember thinking that it could not be that easy. "Don't I have to feel something?" I thought. I remember asking the young woman who led me into that prayer "That's it?" and she said, "Yup!" I honestly did not believe her. I thought there had to be a catch, but there was not. Next, I will show you what we must do to finally break free!

Chapter 11:

Re-Establishing Communion with God

"For whosoever shall call upon the name of the Lord shall be saved."
Romans 10:13 King James Version (KJV)

WHAT SHOULD WE do with all of this information? How can we know for sure that we are going to heaven when we die, and how do we start to hear from God?

We need to come to Jesus and ask him into our heart. We also must be water baptized in a Christian church (not the Catholic Church) by an ordained pastor who was called by God to preach. Do not go to just any pastor; most of them are led by the Catholic Church and are named 'Christian' when they are not.

I will have baptisms in Fort Lauderdale, Florida, and will provide dates on my website if you are interested. To be born again, all we have to do is call on the name of Jesus Christ and ask him to save us, but baptism should be done after we have confessed our belief in Jesus Christ.

If you were baptized as a baby or have been given a head sprinkle or head washing, I cannot stress enough how much I recommend asking God to forgive you and asking him to save you and then getting re-baptized in the proper manner. Baptism does not save us; calling on the name of the Lord Jesus does. However, whenever anyone in the Bible called on the name of the Lord Jesus, they immediately got baptized—almost all the time.

For baptisms in South Florida, please check our site *www.themaskofdeception.org* for dates and locations. There will be an ordained pastor investigated by this ministry and called by God to baptize you and your loved ones. If you cannot attend, please call Christians United for the Freedom of Nations and we will try to find you an approved pastor in your area.

If you cannot make it to one of our baptisms on the beach, do not worry. You can go into a private room in your home, shut the door and ask Jesus to be your God. Ask him to forgive you of your sins and to fill you with his Spirit.

The best way to hear from God is by reading the Bible. The one I suggest is the King James Version, not the New King James Version. Seek God with all of your heart, mind, body, and soul and he will draw near to you:

"And ye shall seek me, and find me, when ye shall search for me with all your heart."
Jeremiah 29:13 King James Version (KJV)

There are five things we must know and believe in our heart and one thing we MUST do to know for sure that we will go to heaven when we die. The Bible does say that we can know for sure that we are going to heaven when we die. It is clear that we can know.

The Bible, God's Word, declares in 1 John 5:13 KJV:

*"These things have I written unto you that believe on the name of the Son of God; **that ye may know that ye have eternal life** and that ye may believe on the name of the Son of God."*

What We Already Know

WE ARE ALL aware of three things:

1. **We are all sinners.** We have all done wrong. Romans 3:10 KJV says, "As it is written, There is none righteous, no, not one."
2. **God is Holy.** The Bible says that God is a Holy, Righteous God. 1 Peter 1:16 KJV "Be ye holy; for I am holy."
3. **One day we will stand before that righteous God to be judged.** Hebrews 9:27 KJV, "And as it is appointed unto men once to die, but after this the judgment:"

The Gospel ("Gospel means Good News")
The good news is that we do not have to pay for our sins and burn in hell. Jesus is God in human flesh, and He canceled our debt.

In Revelation 1:8 KJV, Jesus said:

"I am Alpha and Omega, the beginning and the ending, saith the Lord, which is, and which was, and which is to come, the Almighty."

Here, Jesus claimed to be the God-man. Jesus came to earth to die in our place and pay for our sins. Our debt is canceled, paid in full. He paid the price we should have paid. Do you see how much he loves us? If we do not call on him to save us, then we are not his child yet, and if we die before calling on him, the Bible says we will go to hell.

Jesus did all the work for us, but we must call upon him to save us. Jesus left his throne and his kingdom in heaven for us and became a human being so that his perfect blood would be the final atonement for our sins.

Do not let his suffering go to waste; hell was not intended for us. Hell was designed for the devil and his angels. By God's grace and mercy, he made salvation simple, not complicated. Call on the name of the Lord Jesus, and we will be saved, delivered and set free. Then, get baptized and take communion with your new brothers and sisters in Christ. There are no other ordinances in the Bible, only baptism and communion. Jesus died 2,000 years ago—way before we were born, way before we ever sinned.

"But God commendeth his love toward us, in that, while we were yet sinners, Christ died for us."
Romans 5:8 King James Version (KJV)

Three days later, Jesus rose from the dead and was seen by more than five hundred eyewitnesses at one time.

"And that He was seen of Cephas, then of the twelve: After that, He was seen of above 500 brethren at once; of whom the greater part remain unto this present, but some are fallen asleep."
1 Corinthians 15:5 King James Version (KJV)

He then went back into heaven, where he reigns as the one true God. He is waiting for us to call upon him.

There is only one thing we **MUST do**.

We must ask Jesus to save us, admit that we are a sinner and ask him to give us eternal life. Knowing about Jesus and what he did for you is not enough. Knowledge does not save us. There has to be a point in your life where we can remember that we specifically asked Jesus to save us and fill us with the Holy Ghost.

"That if thou shalt confess with thy mouth the Lord Jesus, and shalt believe in thine heart that God hath raised him from the dead, thou shalt be saved. For with the heart man believeth unto righteousness; and with the mouth confession is made unto salvation. For whosoever shall call upon the name of the Lord shall be saved."
Romans 10:9-10, 13 King James Version (KJV)

For those of you who wish to give your life to the Lord Jesus Christ, say a simple prayer like the following out loud: (not in your mind, please):

Dear Lord Jesus,

I confess that I am a sinner, and that you took my sins on the cross for me. I believe that You died for my sins. I believe that You were buried and that You rose from the dead and are resurrected and alive. I thank You for salvation and ask that You come into my heart to live with me forever and ever. Fill me with the Holy Spirit and take me with you to heaven when I die. I pray that You save my whole family as well.

Amen.

I hope and pray that you make the right decision and that I will see you in heaven one day.

May God bless you and keep you always.

Marisol Pareja

More Information

To find out more about what you've read in The Mask of Deception, for related teachings or messages, for other teachings and insight from Marisol Pareja, or for more about salvation and getting baptized or how to be part of God's work and end-time purposes, write to:

> Christians United for the Freedom of Nations
> 1261 North Lakeview Avenue
> Unit J411 Anaheim, CA 92807
> USA
> You can also visit Marisol's websites:
> www.themaskofdeception.org

Marisol's mission is to help countries and people become free through belief in Jesus Christ. Webinars can be found on the website above.

If you have decided to give your life to Jesus and turn from idol worshiping because of this book or this ministry, we would be interested in hearing your testimony and interviewing you for Marisol's next book and placing your testimony online. We would love to give you a chance to tell others all that Jesus is doing for you since your conversion.

I also make a sincere plea to any priests, nuns, cardinals, bishops or any other clergy from the Catholic Church who would like to come forth and be converted and born again. Please do so as soon as possible. We would love to write about you and your testimony. We would like to add your testimony to the next version of this book. Please contact us:

Email: info@themaskofdeception.org
(all emails confidential)

MORE INFORMATION:
Become a Partner with CUFN
Christians United for the Freedom of Nations

We would also like to invite you to become a partner with CUFN (Christians United for the Freedom of Nations). Your partnership helps us fund our ministry so that we can help countries like Cuba, Haiti, China, and Africa, and India become free from idol worshiping and become free nations again.

Your monthly partnership will be placed into fertile ground so that hundreds and thousands of people all around the world can be forever changed and transformed when they free themselves from idol worshiping and turn to the one true God, Jesus the Messiah.

We will also send you free Bible study materials via email and give you access to a video library on our website to disciple you into becoming a true follower of Jesus Christ.

Thank you for reading my book and may God Bless You,

Marisol Pareja – Founder CUFN

NOTES

John 3:17 KJV

Author Notes
1. Romans 8:17 KJV
2. Psalm 34:17 KJV
3. Romans 3:22 KJV
4. 1 Timothy 2:5 KJV
5. Ekman, Paul, and Maureen O'Sullivan. "Who Can Catch a Liar?" American Psychologist 46, no. 9 (1991): 913-20.
6. Romans 13:11 KJV
7. 2 Corinthians 11:14-15 KJV
8. The Matrix. Performed by Keanu Reeves. United States: Warner Bros. Pictures, 2001. Film.
9. Ephesians 2:8-9 KJV
10. Deuteronomy 7:9 KJV
11. Isaiah 45:5-6 KJV
12. John 14:6 KJV
13. Exodus 34:14 KJV
14. Matthew 11:28 KJV
15. Deuteronomy 4:2 KJV
16. Deuteronomy 12:32 KJV
17. Revelation 22:19 KJV
18. Psalm 12:6 KJV
19. Psalm 119:89 KJV
20. Proverbs 30:5-6 KJV
21. Romans 3:23 KJV

Chapter 1
1. Matthew 7:7 KJV
2. Matthew 18:20 KJV
3. Matthew 10:37 KJV
4. Pareja, Marisol. My Escape from Organized Religion. North Miami Beach, FL: Testimony Publishing, 2015.
5. Exodus 22:18 KJV
6. Simpson, Connor. "Human Skulls Have a Habit of Popping Up at Florida Airports." The Wire. April 24, 2013. Accessed August 31, 2015. http://www.thewire.com/national/2013/04/human-skulls-Florida-airport/64558/.
7. Desmangles, Leslie Gérald. The Faces of the Gods: Vodou and Roman Catholicism in Haiti. Chapel Hill, NC: University of North Carolina Press, 1992.
8. Ephesians 5:11 KJV
9. Ephesians 2:8 KJV
10. McLaughlin, Erin. "Shipment of 18 Human Heads Shipped From Italy Held at Chicago Airport." ABC News. January 15, 2013. Accessed August 31, 2015.

Chapter 2
1. Romans 6:23 KJV
2. Revelation 12:7-12 KJV
3. John 3:16 KJV
4. Genesis 49:17 KJV
5. Luke 23:43 KJV
6. Luke 16:19-31 KJV
7. Revelation 20:11-15 KJV
8. Revelation 21-22 KJV
9. Luke 22:63 KJV
10. Mark 14:65 KJV
11. Apostolic Journey - United States of America: Vespers with the Clergy, Men and Women Religious at St Patrick's Cathedral (New York, 24 September 2015) | Francis http://w2.vatican.va/content/francesco/en/homilies/2015/documents/papa-francesco_20150924_usa-omelia-vespri-nyc.html
12. Isaiah 53:12 KJV
13. Isaiah 53:5 KJV
14. John 19:30 KJV
15. 1 Corinthians 15:6 KJV
16. John 20:27 KJV
17. Luke 24:39 KJV
18. John 20:20 KJV
19. Passion of the Christ, The. Directed by Mel Gibson. 2004. Los Angeles, CA: Newmarket Films, 2004. Film.

20. Romans 5:8 KJV
21. James 2:10 KJV
22. Galatians 3:24-26 KJV
23. Romans 3:10 KJV
24. 2 Peter 3:9 KJV
25. Ezekiel 18:23 KJV

Chapter 3
1. Hebrews 4:12 KJV
2. THE TRUE FACE OF THE ROMAN CATHOLIC INQUISITON -- ROTTEN SPIRITUAL FRUIT FROM THE ABYSS OF HELL
   http://www.cuttingedge.org/news/n1676.cfm
3. "Heretics." In The Catholic Encyclopedia - An International Work of Reference on the Constitution, Doctrine, Discipline and History of the Catholic Church, 368-69. Vol. XVII. New York City, NY: Encyclopedia Press, 1922.
4. Exodus 20:5 KJV
5. Daniels, David W. Answers to Your Bible Version Questions. Ontario, California: Chick Publications, 2003. Chapter 1 page 34
6. Daniels, David W., and Jack T. Chick. "Constantine - The Last Caesar." In Did the Catholic Church Give Us the Bible? The True History of God's Words, 47-49. Ontario, Calif: Chick Publications, 2005. 1.
7. Acts 8:37 KJV
8. Matthew 18:11 KJV
9. Mark 15:18 KJV
10. 1 Peter 1:25 KJV
11. Matthew 24:35 KJV
12. 2 Timothy 3:16 KJV
13. Matthew 23:9 KJV
14. Revelation 17:5 KJV
15. Colossians 2:8 KJV
16. Isaiah 40:22 KJV
17. Job 26:7 KJV
18. 2 Timothy 3:16 KJV
19. 2 Peter 1:20-21 KJV
20. John 3:16, 14:6 KJV
21. Acts 4:12 KJV
22. Isaiah 40:28 KJV
23. Isaiah 43:15 KJV
24. 1 John 2:5 KJV
25. 2 Timothy 3:16 KJV
26. LaHaye, Tim F., and Edward E. Hindson. Exploring Bible Prophecy from Genesis to Revelation. Eugene, Or.: Harvest House Publishers, 2011.

27. Miller, Stephen M., and Robert V. Huber. The Bible: A History: The Making and Impact of the Bible. North American Ed. Intercourse, Pennsylvania: Good Books, 2004.
28. 1 Corinthians 15:6 KJV
29. Luke 24:33-37 KJV
30. 1 Corinthians 15:3-7 KJV
31. Ephesians 2:8-9 KJV

Chapter 4
1. John 20:16-18 KJV
2. 2 Timothy 3:12 KJV
3. Romans 1:16 KJV
4. 2 Corinthians 13:5 KJV
5. James 5:20 KJV
6. 1 Corinthians 11:23 KJV
7. "Easter." Wikipedia. September 10, 2015. Accessed September 14, 2015.
8. "First Council of Nicaea." Wikipedia. September 9, 2015. Accessed September 14, 2015.
9. The Catholic Encyclopedia. New York: Appleton, 1907. Pg. 225,228
10. 1 Corinthians 5:7 KJV

Chapter 5
1. Exodus 20:2-5 KJV
2. "Museum Theme: Vodun." Museum Theme: Vodun. February 3, 2002. Accessed September 14, 2015.
3. Judges 18:30-31 KJV
4. Genesis 49:17 KJV
5. "Vodun." The Ouidah Museum of History. Accessed June 24, 2016. http://www.museeouidah.org/Theme-Vodun.htm.
6. L'Osservatore Romano, February 6, 1993, p.4
7. Judges 17:9-13 KJV
8. 2 John 1:10-13 KJV
9. Chiniquy, Charles. 50 Years in The Church of Rome
10. Ephesians 5:11 KJV
11. Revelation 18:4, 18:8 KJV
12. 2 Corinthians 11:13-14 KJV
13. John 4:24 KJV
14. Exodus 20:3 KJV
15. Galatians 6:7 KJV
16. Exodus 34:14 KJV
17. Deuteronomy 6:14-15, 12:3-4, 4:2, 12:32 KJV
18. Revelation 22:18-19 KJV
19. Exodus 32:1-9 KJV
20. Matthew 15:9 KJV

21. Colossians 2:18 KJV
22. Exodus 20:5-6 KJV
23. John 4:24 KJV
24. Matthew 15:9 KJV
25. Mark 7:9 KJV
26. Revelation 2:6, 2:15 KJV
27. "Situation Summary Data Published on 14 September 2015." Ebola Data and Statistics. September 14, 2015. Accessed September 14, 2015.
28. Jeremiah 31:32 KJV
29. Psalm 33:12 KJV
30. Leviticus 20:13 KJV
31. Deuteronomy 11:17 KJV
32. James 3:1 KJV
33. Matthew 5:19 KJV
34. John 3:3 KJV
35. Exodus 20:1-17 KJV
36. Deuteronomy 5:6-21 KJV
37. "The Second Commandment-Catechism of the Catholic Church." La Santa Sede. Accessed June 26, 2016. http://www.vatican.va/archive/ENG0015/_P7H.HTM.
38. Exodus 20:3-5 KJV
39. "Religious Display and the Courts." The Pew Forum on Religion& Public Life, June 2007, 1. http://www.pewforum.org/files/2007/06/religious-displays.pdf.
40. Romans 3:4 KJV
41. Proverbs 6:16-19 KJV
42. Romans 3:10 KJV
43. Daniel 1-3 KJV
44. Daniel 3:16-18 KJV
45. Matthew 24:24 KJV
46. Philippians 2:10-11 KJV

Chapter 6
1. 2 John 1:10-11 KJV
2. Revelation 22:19 KJV
3. Dash, J. Michael. Culture and Customs of Haiti, 51, 53.
4. "Papa Doc's Concordat (1966)." Concordat Watch. June 12, 1861. Accessed September 14, 2015.
5. Revelation 13:16 KJV
6. Revelation 13:16 KJV
7. "Full Text of Pope's Welcoming Speech in Ecuador." Www.romereports.com. July 6, 2015. Accessed June 26, 2016.

http://www.romereports.com/2015/07/06/full-text-of-popetms-welcoming-speech-in-ecuador.
8. Deuteronomy 4:19, 17:3 KJV
9. 2 Kings 23:5 KJV
10. 1 Corinthians 10:21 KJV
11. Luke 11:23 KJV
12. 1 Timothy 4:1 KJV
13. 2 Thessalonians 2:3-8 KJV
14. Hector, Papa. "Las 21 Divisiones ~ Dominican Vodou." Las 21 Divisiones Dominican Vodou. February 3, 2012. Accessed September 14, 2015.
15. Ezekiel 20:31 KJV
16. Louis, Andre J. Voodoo in Haiti: Catholicism, Protestantism and a Model of Effective Ministry in the Context of Voodoo in Haiti. Mustang, Oklahoma: Tate Publishing & Enterprises, 2007. 1-20.
17. "Lave Tet." Accessed April 22, 2015, http://www.ezilikonnen.com/services/lave-tet.html.
18. Matthew 23:9 KJV
19. Luke 2:22 KJV
20. Ephesians 6:4 KJV
21. Proverbs 22:6 KJV
22. Acts 2:38-40 KJV
23. Matthew 3:16 KJV
24. John 14:26 KJV
25. John 14:16-18 KJV
26. Matthew 12:31 KJV
27. 1 Corinthians 2:12-13 KJV
28. Revelation 18:2 KJV
29. Salvucci, Raul. "Increase in Cases of Demonic Possession." Increase in Cases of Demonic Possession. August 4, 1999. Accessed September 14, 2015.
30. Louis, Andre J. Voodoo in Haiti: Catholicism, Protestantism and a Model of Effective Ministry in the Context of Voodoo in Haiti. Mustang, Oklahoma: Tate Publishing & Enterprises, 2007. 1-20.
31. Matthew 6:9 KJV
32. Matthew 24:24 KJV
33. Matthew 10:30 KJV
34. Hebrews 4:13 KJV
35. Jeremiah 23:24 KJV
36. John 19:26-28 KJV
37. Matthew 10:33 KJV
38. Rigaud, Milo. Secrets of Voodoo. San Francisco, California: City Lights Books, 1985.
39. Genesis 3:4 KJV
40. Matthew 22:14 KJV

41. Luke 1:38 KJV
42. Mazza, Ed. "Pope Francis Credited with Performing Miracle as St. Gennaro's Blood Liquefies." Huffington Post, March 23, 2015. Accessed May 24, 2016. http://www.huffingtonpost.com/2015/03/22/pope-francis-miracle_n_6920624.html.
43. Corbett, Bob. "INTRODUCTION TO VOODOO IN HAITI." Haiti: Introduction to Voodoo. March 1988. Accessed May 24, 2016. http://faculty.webster.edu/corbetre/haiti/voodoo/overview.htm.
44. Watson, Traci. "Jamestown Leaders, 400-year-old Artifact Unearthed." USA Today. July 29, 2015. Accessed September 14, 2015.Numbers 19:13
45. Numbers 19:13 KJV
46. Goodwin, Michele. "Black Markets and Organs." In Black Markets: The Supply and Demand of Body Parts, 189. New York, New York: Cambridge University Press, 2006.
47. Elijah, Samuel. "More than 100 Graves Robbed in Benin for Voodoo Rituals." Reuters. November 30, 2012. Accessed September 14, 2015.
48. Isaiah 8:19 KJV
49. Numbers 9:6 KJV
50. Luke 24:5 KJV
51. Romans 8:17 KJV

Chapter 7
1. Luke 1:38 KJV
2. Matthew 13:55-56 KJV
3. Matthew 12:46 KJV
4. John 2:12 KJV
5. Luke 1:46-47 KJV
6. Luke 2:24 KJV
7. Luke 11:27 KJV
8. Luke 11:28 KJV
9. Deuteronomy 18:10-12 KJV

Chapter 8
1. Revelation 17:4 KJV
2. Daly, John. "The Heresies of Vatican II." The Heresies of Vatican II. April 10, 2014. Accessed September 15, 2015. http://www.holyromancatholicchurch.org/heresies.html.
3. Wikipedia contributors, "Second Vatican Council," Wikipedia, The Free Encyclopedia, https://en.wikipedia.org/w/index.php?title=Second_Vatican_Council&oldid=680906922 (accessed September 15, 2015).
4. Matthew 10:33 KJV
5. Matthew 7:19-21 KJV

6. Matthew 7:18 KJV
7. John 14:6 KJV
8. 1 Corinthians 10:21 KJV
9. Ephesians 2:8 KJV
10. Acts 16:30-31 KJV
11. Byington, Judy. "CAR – Child Abuse Recovery » Catholic Mass Grave Sites of 350,800 Missing Children Found in Ireland, Spain, Canada." CAR – Child Abuse Recovery » Catholic Mass Grave Sites of 350,800 Missing Children Found in Ireland, Spain, Canada. June 7, 2014. Accessed September 15, 2015. http://childabuserecovery.com/catholic-mass-grave-sites-of-350800-missing-children-found-in-ireland-spain-canada/.
12. Tully, Shawn. "The Vatican's Finances (Fortune, 1987)." Fortune. February 17, 2013. Accessed September 15, 2015. http://fortune.com/2013/02/17/the-vaticans-finances-fortune-1987/.
13. Wikipedia contributors, "Catholic Church sexual abuse cases," Wikipedia, The Free Encyclopedia, https://en.wikipedia.org/w/index.php?title=Catholic_Church_sexual_abuse_cases&oldid=680651286 (accessed September 15, 2015).
14. Revelation 17:1-18 KJV
15. Hunt, Dave. "Unholy Alliances." In A Woman Rides the Beast, 215-226. Eugene, OR: Harvest House Publishers, 1994.
16. Bernstein, Carl. "The Holy Alliance." Time, June 24, 2001.
17. Matthew 15:3 KJV
18. Colossians 2:8 KJV
19. Mark 3:24 KJV
20. Matthew 12:25 KJV
21. 2 Timothy 2:15 KJV
22. Cusack, Miss M.F. "Preface." In The Black Pope: A History of the Jesuits, edited by Gerald E Greene. Create Space, 2014.
23. Matthew 7:7-8 KJV
24. 1 Peter 3:22 KJV

Chapter 9
1. Revelation 18:4, 18:8, 18:23, 14:8 KJV
2. 1 Corinthians 11:29 KJV
3. Genesis 3:4 KJV
4. Genesis 3:5 KJV
5. 2 Corinthians 4:4 KJV
6. Wikipedia contributors, "Barack Obama," Wikipedia, The Free Encyclopedia, https://en.wikipedia.org/w/index.php?title=Barack_Obama&oldid=681051309 (accessed September 15, 2015).
7. Wills, G. (2000). Remembering the Holocaust. In Papal Sin: Structures of Deceit (p. 13). New York, New York: Doubleday.

8. Dulles, A., & Klenicki, L. (2001). We Remember a Reflection on the Shoah The Document of the Holy See. In The Holocaust, Never to be forgotten: Reflections on the Holy See's Document "We Remember" (pp. 5-7). New York, New York: Paulist Press.
9. Halmah, Abdull. "Obama, The Pope Meet for First Time - CNN.com." CNN News Article. March 26, 2014. Accessed April 22, 2015. http://www.cnn.com/2014/03/26/politics/obama-pope-meeting-politics/h
10. Ephesians 6:12 KJV
11. 2 Thessalonians 2:4 KJV
12. 1 Thessalonians 4:17 KJV
13. Jeremiah 44:19-22 KJV
14. Exodus 20:3 KJV
15. Ephesians 2:8 KJV
16. Hebrews 9:22 KJV
17. Mark 2:7 KJV
18. 1 Timothy 2:5 KJV
19. Isaiah 44:6 KJV

Chapter 10
1. Deuteronomy 28:1 KJV
2. Psalm 33:12 KJV
3. Leviticus 20:6 KJV
4. Isaiah 45:5, 44:6, 45:21-22 KJV
5. Ezekiel 22:4, 20:31, 23:30, 6:9 KJV
6. "Situation Summary Data Published on 14 September 2015." Ebola Data and Statistics. September 14, 2015. Accessed September 14, 2015.
7. Wikipedia contributors, "Tomás Estrada Palma," Wikipedia, The Free Encyclopedia, https://en.wikipedia.org/w/index.php?title=Tom%C3%A1s_Estrada_Palma&oldid=660703572 (accessed September 15, 2015).
8. Wikipedia contributors, "Fidel Castro," Wikipedia, The Free Encyclopedia, https://en.wikipedia.org/w/index.php?title=Fidel_Castro&oldid=680140283 (accessed September 15, 2015).
9. Hebrews 4:16 KJV
10. John 14:14 KJV

Chapter 11
1. Romans 10:13 KJV
2. Jeremiah 29:13 KJV
3. 1 John 5:13 KJV

What We Already Know
1. Romans 3:10 KJV
2. 1 Peter 1:16 KJV
3. Hebrews 9:27 KJV
4. Revelation 1:8 KJV
5. Romans 5:8 KJV
6. 1 Corinthians 15:5 KJV
7. Romans 10:9-10, 13 KJV

INDEX

50 Years in The Church of Rome 60
Abraham .... xii, 111, 140, 170
Abraham, Isaac, and Jacob 80
Adam and Eve .... x, 14, 15, 133, 157
Africa 53, 55, 58, 73, 90, 175
African 68, 101, 122, 126, 159, 172, 175
Aldert Vrij vii
Altars 100
American Psychologist .... vii, 187
ampulla 124, 125
ampullas 124
ancestors 54, 58, 61, 68
ancestral worship 62
angel of light 61, 62, 63
angels ix, xvi, 14, 15, 18, 60, 65, 75, 108, 127, 133, 135, 144, 151, 157, 158, 173, 174, 176, 182
anointing xi
Anti-Christ 96, 150
Argentina 62
Ark of the Covenant 15, 82
Asia 62
Asian 47, 175
asps 122

Assyrian 97
atheists 40, 58
atonement 15, 182
authority xv, 11, 37, 38, 80, 81, 88, 122, 141, 156
Avery Dulles 159
Baal 55, 97, 111
baby baptism 103
baby dedications 105
Babylon ... 62, 84, 85, 108, 144, 145, 154
backslid 2
Baphomet 97, 110
Baphomet Statue 97
Baptism 11, 103, 106, 180, 182
baptisms 180
baptisms on the beach 180
baptized .... iv, 5, 10, 104, 105, 106, 107, 151, 180, 185
Behanzin 54
believe vii, x, xiii, xiv, xv, 7, 8, 10, 11, 16, 18, 20, 21, 24, 26, 30, 31, 37, 41, 44, 48, 55, 59, 60, 61, 63, 64, 65, 68, 80, 90, 97, 114, 133, 134, 142, 147, 150, 151, 154, 157, 161, 168, 171, 176, 177, 181, 183, 184
believers .. 2, 8, 16, 19, 44, 67, 111, 146, 150
Bella DePaulo vii
black Madonna 60, 119, 120, 150
Black Mary 150
Black Pope 150
blasphemy 145
blessed .... xi, 105, 133, 172, 175
blood 15, 82, 106, 143, 145, 160, 171, 182
Bon Deus 61
Bon dieu 101
born again ..... i, xvi, 7, 8, 10, 27, 45, 111, 123, 147, 180, 186
Buddhism 65, 69, 74
Buddhists 139
Canada 143
Candomble 62
captivity xv, 55, 56, 68, 70, 71, 135, 170, 171
Capuchin Crypt 127
Cardinals 137, 186
Castro 161, 174, 175

Catholic xi, 4, 5, 6, 7, 8, 9, 11, 30, 56, 57, 58, 59, 60, 61, 62, 63, 65, 66, 67, 73, 74, 75, 76, 77, 78, 79, 80, 81, 83, 86, 88, 89, 90, 97, 99, 100, 101, 103, 108, 110, 112, 115, 117, 120, 122, 123, 125, 126, 127, 128, 132, 133, 134, 137, 139, 141, 142, 143, 144, 145, 146, 148, 149, 150, 153, 155, 156, 158, 159, 163, 174, 175, 180, 186, 189
Catholic Church .. 5, 6, 7, 57, 58, 59, 60, 61, 62, 63, 65, 66, 67, 73, 74, 75, 76, 78, 79, 80, 81, 83, 86, 89, 90, 101, 108, 110, 112, 113, 117, 120, 122, 123, 125, 126, 128, 133, 134, 139, 141, 142, 143, 144, 148, 150, 153, 155, 156, 158, 163, 175, 180, 186, 189
Catholicism 8, 53, 55, 60, 61, 69, 73, 75, 88, 90, 98, 99, 100, 101, 104, 119, 123, 125, 145, 151, 159, 168, 174, 175, 192
Charging Bull 97
Charles Chiniquy 60
Chicago, IL 6
child religion 60
children xi, xv, 7, 8, 9, 10, 23, 47, 48, 55, 58, 62, 64, 66, 69, 73, 78, 104, 105, 106, 128, 132, 143, 144, 170
China 48, 69, 70, 170, 174, 175, 186
Christians United for the Freedom of Nations ...... 172, 180, 185, See CUFN
Christmas 63, 95
Commandment ... 64, 67, 77, 78, 80, 82, 83, 135, 147, 170, 172
Communion 106, 179, 182
Communism 60, 69
communist 40, 69, 70, 73, 74, 159, 172, 174, 175
confusion .... ix, 63
consequences .... viii, 37, 101
Consistency 32
contradiction 32
Council of Florence 105
counterfeit viii, ix, xii, 31, 108, 144, 149, 152, 157
crucifiction 57
crucified .... xiii, 16, 17, 18

crucifix 138
crucifixion 17
crypts 6, 96, 125, 127
Cuba 6, 62, 68, 69, 70, 73, 161, 168, 170, 171, 172, 173, 174, 175, 186
Cuban 168, 171, 172, 174, 175
CUFN 186
cults 109
Culture and Customs of Haiti 88
cursed .... xv, 66
Czech Republic 127
Dahomey 54, 101
Dan 54, 55, 56, 57, 58
Dan mark .... See Denmark
Danites 58
Dead Sea Scrolls 32
debt 73, 182
deceive .... viii, ix, xiv, 62, 64, 83, 96, 105, 111, 133, 176
deception vii, viii, ix, 5, 51, 62, 105, 108, 155, 173, 185
declarations 135, 138, 139
decrees 81, 135, 138, 139
defraud ix
Democratic Republic of the Congo 158
demonic 109, 111
demons 7, 60, 80, 94, 109, 122
Denmark 57
denominations 94
Detroit, Michigan 97, 110
devil ... viii, 22, 26, 41, 45, 59, 64, 65, 75, 92, 104, 105, 111, 141, 142, 151, 162, 171, 173, 176, 182
disciples 20, 43, 49, 132
disease 7, 171
diseases 8, 134
disobey 168
doctrines .. 65, 66, 73, 74, 81, 87, 88, 90, 96, 134
Dominican 98, 174
Dominican Republic 98, 174
doubt 1, 156
Dr. Andre Louis 101
drug addictions 123
Earthquakes 69
Easter 5, 43, 45, 48, 49, 50, 63, 67
Easter Bunny 67

Ebola 69, 171
Ecuador 91, 128
ecumenism 138
Egypt 46, 61, 69, 70, 112, 176
Egyptian 68, 122, 128
Egyptians 47, 49, 70, 92, 122
El Papa 102
Elie Lescot 89
enemy ... viii, xi, 45, 63, 75, 97, 105, 110, 116, 137, 142, 158
Erzulie 122, 123, 125
eternity 48, 75
Eucharist 92, 97
Europe 57
eyewitnesses .... ii, 39, 183
Ezili Freda 120
faith ... i, 5, 23, 46, 57, 96, 124, 138, 142, 144, 145
fallen angels 65, 133
fear 21, 137
fellowship .... xii, xiii, 37
Finland 57
First Vatican Council 138
flag 57, 80
flask .... See ampulla
Fon language 56
Fon tribe 54, 58
Francis Loyola 150
Garry Wills 159
genius god .... See Hor-hat
God of the Sun 56
goddess 133
goddesses 60
golden calf 55, 64, 170
governments .... xv, 73, 150
govi jars 124
Gran Soleil 97, 98, 118
graven images 78, 80, 82
graves 126, 127
Great Sun .... See Gran Soleil
Greece 175
Greek 44, 79
guardian god 122
Haiti .. 61, 68, 69, 70, 73, 88, 89, 90, 101, 174, 175, 186, 192
Haitians 98
Halloween 63
healed 38, 48, 134, 167

heals 19
heaven.xii, xv, xvi, 11, 14, 15, 17, 18, 22,
    31, 48, 62, 72, 74, 75, 87, 91, 105,
    116, 133, 134, 139, 151, 153, 165,
    181, 182, 184
hell 9, 16, 18, 46, 47, 60, 62, 75, 105,
    133, 137, 141, 182
Hierophant 112
Hinduism 65, 69
Hindus.. 139
history 19, 25, 26, 28, 38, 40, 48, 49, 56,
    57, 61, 83, 88, 142, 143, 144, 175
Hitler 145
Holocaust 26, 143, 159
holy ... ix, xiv, 33, 37, 50, 76, 81, 88, 108,
    147, 181
Holy Ghost .. i, v, 3, 32, 33, 64, 107, 108,
    111, 132, 138, 162, 183
Holy of Holies 15, 82
Holy See 112
Hor-hat... 122
Horus 112
Iceland 57
idol worshiping ..xi, xvi, 5, 65, 170, 171,
    172, 185, 186
idolatry .... xiii, 55, 56, 78
idols..... xiv, 28, 65, 79, 80, 98, 108, 111,
    168, 170, 172
II Vatican Council 58, 135, 138, 141,
    147, 149
India 69, 70, 170, 186
infallible xv
infant baptism 91
inquisition 150
Intercessor....................................... 151
Ireland... 143
ISIL 150, 160
ISIS 150, 160
Islam ..55, 56, 60, 69, 75, 139, 146, 150,
    159
Israelites ..44, 46, 47, 64, 67, 68, 69, 70,
    78, 82, 84, 128, 170, 172
Italy 6, 61, 109, 125, 144, 188
J. Michael Dash 88
jealous................ xii, 28, 64, 66, 78, 174
Jerusalem 19, 44, 84, 105
Jesuits... 41, 150

Jesus . i, iv, v, vi, vii, x, xii, xiii, xiv, xv, xvi,
    2, 8, 9, 10, 11, 13, 14, 15, 16, 17, 18,
    19, 20, 21, 22, 23, 24, 26, 27, 30, 31,
    34, 38, 39, 40, 41, 43, 44, 45, 46, 47,
    49, 57, 63, 64, 66, 67, 68, 71, 73, 75,
    80, 81, 83, 86, 91, 96, 103, 105, 106,
    107, 108, 110, 111, 114, 116, 117,
    122, 123, 127, 131, 133, 134, 135,
    138, 140, 141, 142, 143, 145, 148,
    150, 151, 156, 162, 167, 168, 173,
    174, 175, 176, 180, 182, 183, 184,
    185, 186
Jewish 49, 50, 51, 85, 143, 150
John Wycliffe...................................... 79
judgment.. 10, 56, 65, 68, 72, 73, 74, 97,
    134, 144, 170, 171, 176, 181
Kanzo... 98
Kenya... 159
King James Bible 75
King James Version 2, 26, 33, 38, 181
Kohen 58
Lady of Sorrows... 100, 121, See Madre
    Dolorosa
Laos 69, 170
Latin 57, 79, 124
Lave Tet.................................... 104, 192
Lazarus 80
Legba 56, 100
Levite... 58
liar .... xv, 81
lies .. vii, x, 22, 39, 49, 65, 133, 141, 171,
    172, 176
Loas... 98
Lucifer 14
Lumen Gentium 141
lying.. 39, 82
Macoutes... 90
Macumba... 62
Madre Dolorosa 120, 122, 123
magic 104, 125, 126, 173, 176
magician.................................. 135, 173
Mary . xv, 11, 43, 44, 45, 80, 83, 85, 105,
    116, 117, 123, 127, 131, 132, 133,
    134, 135, 140, 142
Masonic................................... 110, 111
Masonry 60
mass 124, 160
media................................ vii, 22, 135

mediator 127, 151, 176
mediators 108, 175
mediums .... vii, xi, 108
Messiah 20, 38, 44, 67, 186
Messianic Jewish 67
Methodist 148
Miami Beach, FL 115, 120
Miami Beach, Florida 56, 110, 115
Micah 55, 58
Michelangelo 144
Milo Rigaud 120
miracles 45, 49, 131, 134, 158
Misdirection 173
money 6, 21, 109, 150
Moses 34, 41, 64, 82, 105
Mother Church 60, 148
mummification 128
Muslim 56, 71, 97
Muslims 71, 139, 140
Mussolini 145
My Escape from Organized Religion .. 3
mysteries 98, 112, 145
mystery 61, 144, 146
Mystery Babylon 61, 63
nations ..... xvi, 38, 73, 88, 135, 154, 167, 168, 186
natural disasters 71, 72, 170
Nazism 60
Nebuchadnezzar 84, 85
necromancy . 5, 61, 62, 65, 96, 127, 134, 172, 175
New Jersey 128
New Orleans 68
New World Trade Center 160
New York 97, 125
news .... ii, 127, 159, 182
North Korea 69, 74, 170
obelisk 94, 97
obey 21, 37, 92, 167
occult ...... xi, 9, 57, 90, 96, 106, 110, 112
one world agenda 142, 149
one world religion 149
pagan . 45, 47, 50, 58, 62, 63, 64, 66, 67, 85, 96, 97, 112, 174
pagans 122
Papal Sin 159
Paradise 16

Paraguay 62
Passover ... 44, 45, 46, 47, 48, 50, 51, 95
Pastor 81, 176, 180
Paul 21, 40, 46, 58, 138, 171, 187
pentacle 110
permission 2, 151
persecuting 145
Petro Rite 150
Pharaohs 173
Poland 127
Pope Bom 112
Pope Francis 91, 124, 150, 155, 160, 161, 195
Popes 54, 150, 175
possessed 104, 123
Poteau Mitan 94
power x, 9, 16, 26, 32, 38, 41, 44, 45, 47, 49, 84, 85, 89, 90, 95, 97, 109, 111, 150, 171, 174
prayed 2, 4
prayer 1, 2, 3, 21, 86, 105, 151, 176, 177, 184
prayers .... i, vi, xi, 19, 47, 127, 151
predictions 31, 32, 33
President Bush 158
President Obama 158, 159, 160, 161
priest .. 15, 34, 58, 60, 61, 74, 75, 82, 98, 101, 102, 104, 137, 151
priests 5, 55, 58, 61, 80, 81, 89, 90, 101, 102, 108, 126, 144, 145, 147, 155
promises .... vi, xi, 111
proof xv, 8, 10, 11, 19, 24, 32, 39, 40, 44, 150, 156, 171
prophecy ... xiv, 33, 59, 88, 124, 154, 158
Prophet 140
Protestant 82, 148, 155
psychics .... vii, xi, 108
pyramid 97, 112
Quaker 174
Queen of Heaven 133, 162, 163
Ra 112
Rada Rite 150
Raul Salvucci 109
relationships 123
religion ... iv, xi, xiii, 5, 40, 49, 56, 59, 60, 61, 64, 67, 68, 73, 88, 89, 90, 91,

106, 119, 122, 141, 142, 149, 168, 174, 175
repent 74, 75, 168, 172
reproduce 150
resurrection ...... ii, 16, 26, 44, 45, 46, 47, 48, 49, 95, 131
rewards 16
righteous 16, 17, 23, 83, 181
rites 49, 98, 147
Rome 6, 61, 109, 127, 146, 175
Rosacrucians 57
rules .... xiv, 73, 87
Russia 174
sacraments 11, 22, 106, 182
sacrifice 15, 18, 38, 65, 106, 132
Saint Nicholas .... See Gran Soleil
Saint Patrick's Day 63
Saint Peter's Basilica 94
Saint Valentine's Day 63
Saint Worship 62, 175
saints .... ix, 60, 108, 143, 145, 174, 175
salvation viii, 1, 2, 15, 22, 26, 34, 38, 44, 47, 142, 174, 182, 183, 184, 185
same sex marriage 150
Santa Barbara .... See Black Madonna
Santeria 6, 49, 60, 61, 62, 67, 68, 69, 70, 73, 75, 124, 139, 163, 164, 168, 172, 173, 174, 175
Satan viii, ix, x, xvi, 14, 15, 60, 62, 63, 65, 104, 105, 106, 108, 110, 111, 116, 121, 133, 135, 150, 156, 157, 158, 172, 174, 175
satanic 124, 185
savior 132
scar 121
Science 32
Scotland 57
Scriptures .... ix, 25, 26, 31, 32, 47, 88
Second Commandment 80
Second Vatican Council ... 137, 138, 141, 146
serpent. 16, 55, 56, 57, 60, 82, 100, 121, 122, 156
sickness 7
sin v, x, xv, 13, 14, 15, 18, 21, 22, 23, 46, 47, 74, 75, 79, 83, 96, 132, 133, 134, 162, 170
sinner 183, 184

sins ... v, x, xiii, 15, 17, 21, 40, 46, 47, 62, 83, 107, 153, 168, 180, 182, 184
slavery 76, 150, 174
slaves 170, 175
Spain 128, 143
Spanish Inquisition 26, 143, 146
spire 97
spiritists xi
spirits of the dead 108
spiritual fornication 63
St. Peter's Basilica 57
Statue of Liberty 97
statues ... xiv, 60, 65, 78, 79, 83, 97, 100, 110
steeple 94, 118
Stenio Vincent 89
suffering 161, 182
sun 49, 50, 57, 61, 90, 91, 92, 93, 94, 97, 98, 100, 101, 118, 122
supernatural . xiv, 25, 40, 44, 45, 47, 48, 49, 95, 134
Sweden 57
Switzerland 57
symbol 54, 56, 57, 60, 90, 111, 112, 118, 120, 122, 125
Taoism 61, 62, 69, 74
tarot 108, 112
temples 122
Ten Commandments .... xv, 75, 77, 78
The Matrix .... x, 187
Tomas Estrada Palma 174
torture 57
tradition .. 31, 67, 85, 144, 146, 147, 175
traditions ..... xiv, 48, 58, 65, 66, 97, 147
Trinity 132, 147
truth vii, viii, ix, x, xii, xiii, 7, 8, 26, 37, 38, 39, 41, 46, 47, 48, 49, 58, 63, 65, 66, 75, 80, 81, 83, 89, 107, 124, 133, 141, 146, 149, 150, 156, 157, 171, 173, 176
unbelievers 16
unclean spirits 7, 108, 111
underground cities 61, 127
unfaithfulness 144
United Kingdom 57
United Nations 141
United States 2, 69, 71, 72, 97, 154, 155, 158, 161, 174, 176, 187

Uruguay 62
Vatican 175
Vietnam 69, 170
Voodoo ..... 1, xi, 5, 6, 8, 9, 49, 53, 54, 55, 56, 57, 58, 59, 60, 61, 62, 67, 68, 69, 70, 75, 88, 89, 90, 94, 97, 98, 100, 101, 102, 103, 104, 108, 118, 119, 120, 121, 122, 123, 124, 125, 126, 133, 139, 145, 150, 151, 160, 167, 172, 173, 175, 192
Washington, D.C. 94, 97
West Africa 68, 69, 171, 175
William Tyndale 79
wisdom .... xi, 84, 108, 146
witchcraft 61, 96, 176
Witches 48
witnessed 5, 45
wizards 109, 168
World Council of Churches 142, 149
World Health Organization 68, 171
worship xv, 8, 28, 46, 47, 48, 49, 50, 54, 55, 56, 57, 61, 63, 64, 65, 66, 68, 70, 71, 74, 81, 82, 83, 84, 85, 90, 97, 108, 111, 116, 118, 119, 122, 123, 127, 131, 139, 150, 159, 162, 168, 170, 172, 174, 175
worshiped .... xii, 18, 64, 174
worshiping ...... xi, xiii, 80, 135, 168, 170, 172, 174
Yahweh .... xii, 97, 110, 170, 172
YHVH .... See Yahweh

www.ingramcontent.com/pod-product-compliance
Lightning Source LLC
Chambersburg PA
CBHW050534300426
44113CB00012B/2090